Praise for Lunch with the Lord

While serving in the US Army in the 1980s, I was assigned as a singer to the US Army Band and Chorus, Europe. One of our concerts took us to Como, Italy. We stayed in a local establishment and were afforded the opportunity to eat the most divine Italian cuisine any of us had ever tasted. The hotel staff fed us Soldiers as though we were never going to eat again as long as we lived! Each meal was carefully thought out and caused us to eat...as though we would never eat again!!! And now, my good friend, Laura Padgett, has prepared a meal for you that will feed you as though...

The meals God provides for us are designed to give us the sustenance we need, while at the same time, thrilling our palettes. Each section of Laura's book—*Garnishing with Gratitude; Surrender Salad; The Main Course; The Delights of Dessert*—will cause you to consider the meals God has prepared for you as you move forth in these seasons He has created specifically for you. You will dine on each sumptuous course so that when you finally finish, you will have consumed the sustenance you needed that will cause you to grow, thrive, and flourish at the table God has prepared for you.

Enjoy this meal! It is not a snack! It is so much more than 4 courses...it is healing nourishment for your seasons to come. God bless you!

—Beatrice Bruno, The Drill Sergeant of Life
Author of *How To Get Over Yourself and Let Go of the PAST; God Has Prepared the Table! Why Aren't You Eating?;* and *The Baby Chronicles—Where You Were Before You Were!* (Fiction)

Lunch with the Lord serves up bite-sized stories full of faith, heart, and gentle wisdom. With charm and wit, Laura Padgett invites us to sit at the spiritual table each day and savor God's presence. A fun, uplifting read that leaves you filled—and still wanting more.

—Dawna Hetzler,
Author of *Free to Receive* and *Walls of a Warrior*

Laura Padgett's *Lunch with the Lord* is not just a book—it's a living testimony, a poured-out offering of wisdom, humility, and humor that nourishes the soul like a sacred meal prepared with care. Each page dances between sorrow and joy, hardship and hope, all anchored in the unwavering love of God. Through her poetic storytelling and servant-hearted transparency, Laura invites readers into holy moments of reflection, reminding us that even in grief, laughter, or dishes in the sink, God is speaking. This work is a beautiful extension of Laura's calling. I believe it is a gift for hearts seeking healing, meaning, and presence in the everyday. I am honored to link arms with her in Kingdom purpose and share in the feast she has lovingly set before us. Thankful to be a guest at the table.

—April D. Metzler
Owner, Intentionally Teachable Leaders, LLC
Founder/CEO, Kingdom Industries United, Inc.
Host, RSVP Show Podcast/TV Show
Creator, Pause4Presence Project
Author, Speaker, Songwriter

In *Lunch with the Lord*, Laura Padgett serves us a soul-nourishing feast filled with wisdom, compassion, and comforting reassurance that we are not alone on our journeys. Through heartfelt storytelling and poetry delivered in bite-sized, manageable pieces, she gently encourages us to slow down, breathe, and recognize life's simple moments as sacred opportunities for acceptance, belonging, and connection.

Her words are a balm for the soul—sometimes sparking joyful laughter, other times revealing raw, unresolved issues that flow into streams of gentle healing. Heartfelt and sincere, her reflections inspire us to be open and authentic, recognizing that even in simple or difficult moments, we can learn profound and transformative life lessons.

This book offers more than just words on pages; it creates a sacred space where you can find serenity, hope, and affirmation that we are citizens of the world and members of God's kingdom—loved, accepted, and cherished just as we are. Whether nestled in your online library or displayed on your bookshelf, nightstand, or end table, this inspiring, beautifully written book deserves a special place in your heart. It's a divine invitation to pause, reflect, and immerse yourself in God's grace and love—shown through words that nurture both heart and spirit.

—Gwendolyn Odom,
Author of *You Don't Know Just How I Feel: Hope for the Grieving Heart*

Lunch with the Lord

A Four-Part Banquet of Heart, Mind, and Soul-Nourishing Wisdom

Laura L. Padgett, M.A.

Illustrations by
Sally M. Cordrey, M.A.

ELEVATION PRESS
OF COLORADO

Lunch with the Lord
A Four-Part Banquet of Heart, Mind, and Soul-Nourishing Wisdom

by Laura L. Padgett, M.A.

Illustrations by Sally M. Cordrey, M.A.

Cover and interior design and interior formatting by Donna Marie Benjamin of Elevation Press of Colorado.

Gingham pattern red background on cover by juicy_fish/freepik.com

Plate with spoon and fork icon on cover by freepik.com

Illustrations by Sally M. Cordrey, M.A.; sallycordrey@comcast.net

Author photo by Lu Anne Tyrrell; luanne @coloradoscenes

Praying hands icon: hand drawn design elements collection for palm sunday/freepik.com

THE LITTLE DRUMMER BOY
Words and Music by KATHERINE DAVIS, HENRY ONORATI and
HARRY SIMEONE
© 1958 (Renewed) EMI MILLS MUSIC, INC. and
INTERNATIONAL KORWIN CORP.
Exclusive Worldwide Print Rights Administered by ALFRED MUSIC
All Rights Reserved
Used by Permission of ALFRED MUSIC

All Scripture quotations, unless otherwise indicated, are taken from the Holy Bible, New International Version (NIV), copyright 1973, 1978, and 1984 by the International Bible Society.

Ordering information: Special discounts are available on quantity purchases by book clubs, corporations, associations, and others. For details, contact the author at the address above.

ISBN 978-0-932624-40-6

1. Main category — [Religion] 2. Other categories — [Inspirational]

ELEVATION PRESS
OF COLORADO

www.elevation-press-books.com

Contents

For Mary, my wee sister,
who went home before me.
And my life became stillness,
I could neither hear nor see.

I cried many tears and then,
my vision washed clear.
I turned around, turned around,
seeing that she is still here.

So, I picked up my pen,
as she would wish me to do.
As I danced along these pages,
she said "Sister, I believe in you."

—*Mary Lorene Carvallo 1953–2024*

Acknowledgements

In more than a decade as a professional author, I've been blessed to know many different authors. In that time, I have never known one author to say they birthed a book baby all by themselves. So it is with this book baby. There are more people than I can name here who have contributed to this work. But I would like to thank a few of them publicly, in print.

My husband Keith is that voice of reason when I am discouraged in my artistic endeavors. He holds me when I cry, endlessly encourages me when I face doubts (from others and especially from myself), and never complains when it seems I have taken up residence at my keyboard. He is, more often than he knows, the inspiration for much of my inspiration.

As with my other two books, these stories are enhanced by the fine art abilities of my dear friend, Regis University Colleague, Alpha Sigma Nu sister, partner in prayer, and fellow lover of the dance, Sally Cordrey. She is a visionary in art and in life. She married my ideas with hers to create graphics of a delicious meal. Her work never fails to make my work better.

My friend, Jeanette DeQuinze, is a beautiful soul who visits my booths at events, encourages me, and has walked with me in the grief journey I am still on. When I told her of my idea to do this third book, based on daily walks with God, she suggested that I start from the lens of gratitude. She was right.

My friend Debbie Blanchard kept me on track by helping me understand it might just be time to make this book dream a reality. She never pushed nor tried to convince me to move forward after my sister Mary's death. Instead, she understood my grief and gently provided space to find my way back to my calling.

My friendship with Lu Anne Tyrrell, the photographer who supplied my author picture on the back of this book, is proving to be a treasure. While spending time trying to get the right lighting, positioning, and atmosphere, she taught me how to wait on Mother Nature with patience, flexibility, and grace.

I was careful when enlisting help from beta readers. Those are the people who saw this work in its raw form and offered suggestions to tighten and increase the meaning of my stories. I counted on them for honesty and gentle critiquing to create a book we can look upon with pride. Those ladies are Connie Pittenger, Sharon Hayes, Linda Pavlich, and Heather Pearce. Thank you, friends.

I am humbled by the endorsements given here by women of artistic accomplishments well beyond my own. I am grateful they have taken time to review this work and have given it a stamp of approval from their generous artistic hearts. That means more to me than I can express here. But I can offer, "Thank you, Sisters," to Beatrice Bruno, Dawna Hetzler, April Metzler, and Gwendolyn Odom.

Foreword

Laura Padgett is delightful, vibrant, and someone you want to know. In her book *Lunch with the Lord,* she's inviting you to sit with her at her table, drinking your favorite coffee or tea, and share a meal as she shares stories that draw you in and give you a peek into her life and her walk with Jesus.

Laura doesn't just write devotionals; she opens the door wide and welcomes you into sacred conversations, ones that feel personal and full of grace. She has a storyteller's heart and a teacher's gift. Through her words, you'll find laughter, tenderness, and deep spiritual insights woven seamlessly into everyday moments. Her voice is warm and wise, grounded in faith and lived experience.

Each chapter is like a lovingly prepared dish, seasoned with Scripture and garnished with honesty, humor, and hope. You're not just reading reflections; you're partaking in nourishment for the soul. One such chapter, *"Garnishing with Gratitude,"* shows her heart so beautifully. It's more than a metaphor. It's a way of life. A gentle invitation to shift perspective, to see even the "less desirable" moments through the lens of God's goodness.

Laura reminds us, we each have a choice every morning: to start our day in a posture of complaint or of praise. Her encouragement is never preachy. Instead, it's a quiet nudge, like a friend who lovingly reminds you to slow down and savor the presence of the Lord in the ordinary.

Lunch with the Lord isn't just a devotional, it's a companion. One that helps you frame, refocus, and return to the table of grace, again and again. What a gift. And what a joy it is to share in Laura's journey and welcome her words into your heart.

—Karen DeArmond Gardner, Pastoral Trauma Coach and author of *Hope for Healing from Domestic Abuse.*

Introduction

A physician once lectured me on the nutritional value of food choices. He insisted that a meal is just for sustenance and body maintenance. To him, it was that simple. Looking back now, I think I must have given the impression that English was not my first language, that I was applying for admission into the farm for the bewildered, or I was silently questioning his mental stability. None of those scenarios were true. I couldn't blame him, because I sat blinking as if my eyes were dilated and I was staring into a 400-watt light bulb. I simply couldn't imagine seeing meals through such a simplistic, minimized lens.

As a youngster, I learned the art of cooking from my Sicilian-American father. Meal preparation was a well-choreographed, multi-part production. His culinary endeavors were offered with the flare of a five-star restaurant. Each part was carefully planned and presented, whether a Christmas dinner or a simple dish of left over pasta and beans (pasta fagioli). To Papa, and now to me, a meal is a feast.

As I grow older, I see life in that same way. I find it to be a dish served each day with multiple parts and diverse lessons to savor. I have tried to craft these lessons into this four-part representation of living life in the loving care of God. It is my belief that the Father of everyone presents living as more than merely existing. I have learned that, like my earthly father, God offers His children a feast to be savored as He teaches, sustains, guides, and gifts each of us.

May you find this meal satisfying for your heart, soul, and mind. And may you always choose to see life as a divine table set before you to enjoy while inviting others to share with you.

—Laura L. Padgett

Part One

Garnishing with Gratitude

As a child, I stood next to my Sicilian-American father as he crafted culinary creations using memories from his ethnic background. He told me that it isn't enough to just place a dish on the table for consumption. In his opinion, food must be as appealing to the eyes as it is to the taste buds. He emphasized garnishing with elements that would invite the recipient into the meal. He once told me that, even a meal that does not seem to be desirable, can be made so with the use of the proper garnish.

I often reflect upon these kitchen lessons from my earthly father. I find many of the techniques he taught are useful in navigating daily living.

For example, when I start my day, I can garnish it with grudges, anger about the things I am trying to control but failing, hurt feelings, fears, or insecurities. Or I can get out of bed in a posture of gratitude, thanking God for the very breath that signals I awakened to another day.

When I choose to garnish each day with gratitude, I am more likely to embrace, with grace, what has been placed upon my plate, appealing or not. Filling my conscious mind with a tank of "Thank You, Lord," makes my days more palatable. This is true regardless of my circumstances, physical or spiritual trials, annoyances, or when struggling to put my human ego on hold while learning lessons from the great Master.

The Next Right Step
When gratitude guides the journey

"I have spent most of my life behind bars. Many people see me as hard and scary. In some ways, I guess I am. Others see me as an unfortunate member of society who fell on hard luck. Still others feel I am just lazy and find life easier by living off taxpayers' money in prison. In all honesty, I can't say I ever met anyone who woke up one day and decided it would be a blessing to spend part of their life in jail.

But for me it was a gift, because it was there I became a believer in the risen Christ. Today I live in joy and hope. And I am free in more ways than I can count," he said.

The speaker was a member of our adult Sunday School class and up to this point no one knew of his past. Normally, he spoke very little. That day, we were studying gratitude. It was then he chose to share his story.

"You see," he told us, "As a kid I learned that stealing was okay and using whatever means I could to eat was just a matter of survival."

No one in the room spoke. I hoped our silence would encourage him to continue speaking. It did.

"The first time I was in jail, I learned very little except how to stay alive and perfect my criminal techniques for when I got outside those cold walls. I was young and hung on every word uttered by the seasoned offenders."

He let the hush linger in the room. When he continued, his audience hung on **his** every word.

"The second time I was imprisoned, for the same type of crime, I was in solitary confinement because I picked fights with, and stole from, other inmates. It was in that dark hole of loneliness and isolation that the prison chaplain introduced me to Jesus Christ and His forgiveness. The Chaplain encouraged me to read a Bible he left with me, along with a small flashlight to illuminate the words before me.

As I studied and learned of Christ's mercies and promise of a new way to live, I felt something I had never known—gratitude. It did not happen overnight. Eventually, with nothing else to do and with truly nothing else to lose, I opened my heart to the message in the book I had been given. Even I, a career criminal, who had only taken from society, was loved and welcomed into the flock of Jesus.

After release from solitary confinement, I was returned to my cell. Every day when I awoke, I made my way across five feet of cold floor to the lavatory. I began to speak with each step. When I put my right foot down, I said 'Thank' and when I put my left foot down, I uttered 'You.'

Soon it became a ritual for me to walk with those two words in my mind and feet throughout my day. 'Thank you. Thank you.'

This simple act allowed me to weather the harsh prison environment until my release. And today when I get up, I still walk to the bathroom, in my small apartment, with those same steps and words of gratitude."

I asked him how he finds life on the outside. He said most days are good, even though he has challenges and roadblocks because of his past decisions. He confessed that many times he is not sure what he needs to do, and is tempted to return to what he once knew as existence options.

"But," he said, "one thing is for sure. When I remember the sacrifice Jesus made for me so I could live hopeful and free, I cannot help but start my day thanking and praising Him. Then, no matter what or who I meet, if I walk in thankfulness, I am taking the next right step."

Today's Prayer

Lord, as I start each day, please help me to be willing to step into my life with these two important words, "Thank You."

Well, Maybe

Inconvenience: another word for classroom

"I have bad and good news," my husband informed me one day when I returned from an exercise class. "The bad news is the dishwasher just quit."

"What's the good news?" I asked.

Keith continued, "I think it's just a matter of a small part that we can replace, and I can fix it, maybe. But it will take at least a week to get the part."

I sighed. This is a first world problem and no more than a minor one at that. Still, I am now and always have been grateful for my Mr. Fix-It mate. So, I resigned myself to a week of washing dishes by hand and waiting for the part that was the cure for the ailing dishwasher, maybe.

"I have bad news and good news," Keith told me a week later. The good news is the part arrived two days earlier than expected. The bad news is it did not fix the issue. "I guess we must buy a new dishwasher. We'll have to start shopping."

Each place Keith looked online or in the stores, he found that the dishwasher we wanted was not in stock and had to be ordered. The best we could hope for was a six-week delivery date, maybe.

Then I remembered we had made another purchase from a small appliance store here in our town. We decided to go and see what they had available. They had just the right one for us in their warehouse. They estimated a delivery date within a week, maybe. We purchased the appliance, waited and washed dishes by hand for another week.

Because there are just the two of us at most meals in the Padgett household, we let the dishes pile up throughout the day and then washed them together at night. It was in this simple (what many now consider primitive) daily chore, we found a lovely blessing.

In the evening, in our small kitchen, by a large window looking out into our yard, we had time to look at (and really see) springtime delights popping up all around us. For me, the evening hours have always afforded times of peace and reflection—an escape from the daily rush of activities.

One week turned into two and then three. Each evening, we moved around our small kitchen, washing and drying dishes. Many times, we were in silence, many times in light conversation. We enjoyed the hummingbirds' exquisite choreography in the twilight hours. We moved around each other in response to the peaceful rhythms of day's end. Each lazy sunset brought more intense greenery and small, early spring flowers into view.

We still had a couple of delays peppered with apologies and promises of, "Tomorrow, maybe." We chose not to tumble into the trap of urgency that informs us we must always be moving on to the next task. We just kept washing and drying dishes, watching, breathing, and enjoying the moments.

When the dishwasher finally arrived, the delivery man installed the appliance, checked to make sure it worked and handed us the paperwork for our purchase. As he exited our house, he smiled and said, "Well, I bet you'll be excited to use your new dishwasher. No more washing dishes by hand, huh?"

As he pulled out of the driveway, I reflected on his last words about abandoning the hand washing chore each night. Then I remembered the peace and harmony in our new evening ritual and muttered to myself, "Well, maybe."

Today's Prayer

Father God, I am not always able to slow my pace and take in lessons or beauty of your offerings. I confess this. Thank you in advance for making me willing to put brakes on when I am in danger of by-passing your blessings

The Wrong Number

Treasure of the non-mistake

"Hello Laura," the voice on the other end of the telephone was not the one I expected to hear when I dialed. In fact, I was uncertain who the voice represented. I wondered if I had awakened the person answering the phone.

"Hi. Is this Kathee?" I asked.

"No, it isn't. But I'm so glad you called. I've been thinking I should call you. I was up again all night and scrolling through Facebook when I saw one of your posts. It reminded me that you are one person I really need to connect with because you understand things others just can't. When I saw your number come up on the screen, it was uncanny."

I immediately realized I had dialed the wrong number and pulled the cell phone from my ear to see the display screen. To my surprise, the number listed on the screen did indeed say "Kathee."

"Laura, are you there?" she asked.

"Yes, yes, I'm here. I was just checking something on my phone." I said, "How are you, and what is going on?" I now recognized the voice's owner.

She told me about a situation she had been dealing with in recent days. We have been friends for many years and have formed a close bond, even if we do not talk for a few months at a time. We have multiple things in common including what she needed to share with me today. We are sisters in the journey of pain caused by a loved one.

I said little and just listened. She asked for no advice. I offered none. I learned a long time ago that good friends do not try to fix other people's pain or problems. God does not call us to do that. He calls us to come alongside and stand in the pain with open ears and loving hearts, while suspending judgment and resisting temptation to supply answers so we, ourselves, can find an exit ramp from heartache.

As we talked, I realized that I was meant to connect with this dear friend. We shared stories, honored each other's feelings, and just sat holding one another over the miles in a gentle sway of support and concern.

The conversation lasted well over an hour. I was grateful, not for her situation, but for time to be with another in the common bond often formed by discomfort and uncertainty. When the call ended, I took a couple of minutes to find out how it was I had made this call in the first place.

Apparently, I had put this friend's number under Kathee's name. And while trying to connect with Kathee, God directed me to this friend. I sat in awe of the good Father who wastes no time when sending in the cavalry of support and understanding based in commonality and love. Just as this dear one has always been there to lend an ear and shoulder to me, I was privileged to be those things for her now.

I rested in silent prayer for a long time and then undertook the task of straightening out the phone directory I rely upon for remote communication. I couldn't believe I had made the mistake of putting one number under another person's name. Normally I would have been embarrassed at dialing the wrong number. While pondering this, I remembered what I prayed in my devotional time earlier. I told God I was submitting my day to Him to do what He wanted and asked Him to send me where He needed me to do His work. I smiled in the knowledge that God does not have wrong numbers in His directory.

"Thank you, Lord," I whispered.

Then I left my cell phone on the table, grabbed my car keys, jumped into Lynard, my 1969 VW bug, and headed for the river. I needed silent time to fellowship with the One who arranges meetings that are never by accident.

Today's Prayer

Lord, I thank you for placing people in my life as ministers and those who need to be heard and receive ministering.

Not So Fast

The art of resisting a quick solution

"I can book us on a flight home today, if that's what you want," my husband, Keith, said.

I could hear his voice but was having trouble focusing on him after a night spent with severe motion sickness on our cruise. This was a night for the books! Seriously, I made amends for the last seventy years, made sure my son or granddaughter, Sophia, would get my 1969 VW, and finally fell asleep after taking a motion sickness remedy I found buried at the bottom of my purse. I put it there for, "just in case." Well, that night was in the category of "just in case."

After offering a prayer of gratitude for the ship being docked upon awaking, I told Keith I didn't think we should make that decision so fast until we had a cup of tea. We got dressed and went to the dining room.

There were several people in the breakfast area looking as if they had not weathered the previous night very well either. While eavesdropping (I admit it), I learned that in fact the sea had been rougher than usual that first night of the cruise. When I shared my experience too, there were many voices encouraging me to take Dramamine®. I do not tolerate this product well, but there was no use trying to explain. I felt hopeless as they all insisted this was the only way to go. Their intentions were good. But, that course of action would have rendered me asleep throughout the trip. I felt if that was my only choice, it was best to fly home.

At a table right next to us, sitting by herself, was another lady. I recognized her as she had introduced herself the previous afternoon. Her name was Gosia. She and her husband, Ali, provided entertainment for this cruise. They had been on this cruise before. She had overheard the conversation and understood. She too had a difficult first night. According to her, this cruise was normally smooth, and there were some great sights to see should we choose to stay.

"I am not offering you advice," I heard her say. And she wasn't. She was extending an empathetic ear. I found her gentle nature and sweet countenance alluring. I asked how she copes with working on a ship if she is prone to motion sickness. She shared some of the remedies she found helpful. I listened and realized that there may be a way for me to enjoy my trip without motion sickness or the somnolent state produced by medications.

I took her non-advice and went shopping on shore to collect items such as essential oils and non-drowsy alternative medications for motion sickness, (which I did not know existed). From then on, I did not have any more motion sickness episodes, even on a night when there was more than a little rocking of the ship.

During one of our morning devotional times, Keith and I thanked God for a new friend and the information that prevented us from cutting our trip short. Gosia was right. This turned out to be one of the best experiences of my life. If we had returned home early, we would have missed meeting people we hope will be friends for a long time to come, hours of scenic tours, history lessons, schooner sailing, lobster boating, explorations of military forts, shopping in charming New England towns, and so much more.

To me, one of the best parts of this journey was being entertained by two extremely talented musicians, Gosia and Ali. They not only had us dancing and doing conga lines, but educated us on the history of songs, song writers, genres, and musical time periods. When Gosia found out I am a trained interpretive dancer, she invited me to dance to their rendition of "The Sound of Silence."

After the trip, I pondered my new friend Gosia's words that proved useful in making the right decision. I remembered the way she stood in the discomfort with me, offered no advice but shared her experience, wrapped in empathy.

I pray that I will keep this example before me as I encounter others who may be in a tough spot and not looking for advice but just in need of someone to understand how they feel. Authentic empathy is an effective tool we can offer to others as they figure out their own solutions. I pray that when I am again in a situation of thinking a quick solution is the answer, I will recall the benefits of saying, "Not so fast."

Today's Prayer

Father God, I often get into thinking there is only one way of finding a solution. Please make me willing to examine other options brought to the table, while thanking you and others.

Helga, the Healer

A most unexpected partner on my grief journey

In my family of origin, it was unacceptable for children to have or show emotions. This was true of anger, sadness and especially grief. It was widely believed that children were resilient and unaffected by events or people around them. I grew up in the camp of doing all that was possible to avoid annoying the grown-up types.

I have carried this model with me most of my adult life, and found that often the emotions came out anyway, usually at inappropriate times, places and in extreme proportions. The philosophy of stoically carrying on, however, proved to be useful in early January of 2024 when my best friend and younger sister, Mary, passed away after a brief battle with cancer. As the executor of her will, I had all I could do to contend with estate administration, bill paying, and funeral arrangements. All of this was made more intense in the face of two family members who felt I had not handled things properly. Their words added guilt to the knife-like emotional stabbings begging for my attention.

When the last technical detail was put to rest, I collapsed into a world of mental and sometimes physical despair. I had no idea how to process all I was feeling around this loss.

I turned to a grief counselor who informed me that when we stuff our emotions, they will find a home in our bodies and can make us unwell. She likened grief to a block of cement lodged somewhere between our heart and gut. I understood that analogy as I felt weighed down with emotions that I was sure could be eliminated by just ignoring them. She told me the best thing I could do to honor the memory of my sister was attend to my own emotional, mental, and physical well-being.

Following her advice, I visited my physician for help in bringing my blood pressure back into normal range and hoped he could suggest methods for relieving my incessant heartburn and insomnia. Part of my care plan, along with medications, was to find a grief group. It was there I met people who also were grieving the loss of loved ones. I found that what I was feeling was not at all unusual or abnormal. I began to learn healthy ways to embrace and express my grief.

During one of my darkest days, my husband took me to a Celtic harp concert. Because I had performed, taught, and competed in Irish Dance for over thirty years, he thought the familiar music and lively atmosphere would soothe my broken heart. I went to the leader of the harp group, at the conclusion of the concert, and thanked her for this musical gift. I told her I had danced to many of the songs they offered that day. She invited me to come, teach, and dance with the harp team.

As our relationship developed, I took advantage of a free harp lesson and made the decision to try and play the harp. My teacher sent me home with a loaner harp. I felt we were going to spend quite a bit of time together, so I gave the harp a name. I called her Helga.

Because the harp rests on the harpist's knees, the vibration of the strings, when played, are felt throughout the body. As I practiced scales, chords, and simple tunes, I found the hypnotic music opened a pathway to grieve my loss and address emotions that sat trapped in my body, mind, and heart for several months.

As the lessons and practices continued, the cement block softened and crumbled into manageable blocks of surfacing pain, confusion, sadness, anger and even guilt. I realized these needed to be felt, heard, and honored. I learned to rely upon people who understood what I was living, and the soul-soothing music Helga and I played. Soon, I began going in public again and interacting with friends and family who supported my journey. I also dropped the explanations and defenses I tried offering to my accusers.

Helga demanded nothing of me, did not judge my brokenness or blame me for not being able to contain the flow of tears. There was no set time line that would signal when my grief expression was to cease. She leveled no guilt on me because of decisions I had to make, whether right or wrong. Many days I leaned against Helga as we played and released the watery streams bursting from my grieving heart. She provided a path to take the first steps on the road toward healing from the trauma of loss.

A little over one year since the passing of my sister, I now know that to identify, acknowledge, and express feelings is a natural part of being a loving human. I am grateful to my teacher, Robin Freed, and Helga for showing that to me and helping me leave the old cultural and familial messages behind.

When I decided to get serious about playing harp, I purchased one of my own. That meant, because she was on loan, Helga had to return to the studio. I suppose that like many healers, she was only meant to be my companion for a season. I again felt a plethora of emotions as my new friend left my side. I do, however, take great comfort in the fact that Helga will be lent to someone else for their journey. Perhaps she will help another find a new art form to explore or awaken a dream that has been put aside. I like to think that maybe she will again offer a pathway for the feet of another broken heart to take steps toward finding healing.

Today's Prayer

Lord, please make me willing to see your goodness, health, and healing in the animate and inanimate of this world and to thank you for "all" the ways you send your love and comfort.

The Wee Tree

Embracing simplicity in an extravagant world

When my life fell apart in 1990, due to divorce, with the accompanying emotional and financial disasters that brings, I was determined to try and make life as normal for my small child as possible. As a single mother, in debt and without extra money to spend on Christmas, I fretted over how to purchase a Christmas tree for our little apartment. My neighbor worked at a facility housing battered women and their children. She told me that as a fund raiser, they were selling used artificial trees for the holidays. When entering the sales room, I saw a very small tree in the corner that looked like it had seen better days. It was thin, asymmetrical, and stood out from the other trees due to its odd shape and muted color. It appeared to be completely alone. I was drawn to what I considered a kindred soul in an inanimate object.

I bought the little tree for five dollars and took it home. I had salvaged some meager decorations from previous years and did my best to add a bright spot to what was a strained, sad holiday. I spent that first Christmas, with the little tree, alone as my son was with his father and I had no invitations from family or friends. So, my new found buddy (an artificial three-foot tree) and I spent a quiet day eating a TV dinner and drinking hot apple cider.

I remember that day vividly as the scene still plays out of a newly divorced, single woman with no money, sipping cider, eating a TV dinner, and feeling isolated from holiday festivities as I had once known them. I waited in the apartment for my son to return with his bounty of expensive gifts from his dad and grandparents. I prayed he would not be too disappointed when he opened the one little gift I had purchased for him in a thrift shop the week before.

What, by the world's standards, looked like a miserable holiday turned out to be perhaps one of the best Christmas celebrations I have ever had. That is because during the day I felt God reach down and assure me I was not alone and forgotten. In the forced simplicity of my situation, distractions fell away. It dawned on me that the best part of Christmas is when we accept the true gift of a little child who came to offer hope to the hopeless, comfort to those who feel lost and community to those who believe they are abandoned. Like that little tree, Christ was/is humble and, by all accounts, not flashy or flamboyant on any level.

That was not my last Christmas spent alone. Nor was it the last financially lean situation I have endured. But it was one of the richest and most blessed days of my life. In the stillness and silence of solitude I was reminded that through the good and the not so good times, through the lean and not so lean times and through the happy and not so happy times, several truths are undeniable. I am not now, never have been, and never will be distanced from the lover of my soul. I am now and always have been loved. I possess and always will possess riches beyond measure.

Over the past thirty plus years, I could have replaced the wee tree with a larger and more festive one, adorned with more ornaments and frills. But I have not. I have chosen to keep my friend, the small tree. I have transported it from dwelling to dwelling because it holds more value for me than all the riches someone could offer. It holds the memory of the Christmas Day when God soothed my broken heart, offered me the glimmer of hope, and assured me that the gift He gave on Christmas is the same gift He gives every single day—His love. Nothing large or sparkly can compare to that.

This year after I set up my tiny tree and decorated it with some of the same ornaments from that first, lean Christmas, I sat in my favorite rocking chair in silence and solitude. I was wrapped in a shawl and warmed by the fireplace. In the dark, with just a small string of lights shining, I remembered the great holiday times and the ones that were somewhat sad. I have often heard it said that it is okay to look back but not to stare—and so I do, and I do not. Cradling my cup of hot cider, I wrapped all memories in a ribbon of gratitude and rested in the glowing community and friendship shared by the Lord, the wee tree and me.

Today's Prayer

Father God, help me to see, and thank you, in the lean times as well as in the time of plenty.

Holy Humor Saves the Day
Relief is just a laugh away

Stop and go traffic is not uncommon at any time, on any day, when one travels on a busy Wheat Ridge, Colorado, motorway called Wadsworth Boulevard. Friday afternoons can present stressful driving conditions with traffic congestion. During one Friday I learned a lesson in letting go of a situation, letting God take control and relaxing in the fact that indeed there is a funny side to most things in life.

I was moving at a snail's pace and had given myself plenty of time to deal calmly with the line of brake lights I knew would greet me along my path. I've traveled the Denver Metro Area all my life, and I learned a long time ago the clock is only my friend when I do not try to challenge Father Time with excuses for why I couldn't leave room for possible (probable) delays.

I sat in line with other cars waiting for the light to turn and allow traffic to move a few yards forward, when I heard the screech of brakes. I looked in my rearview mirror and saw an SUV skid to a stop just inches from the rear of my car. With my eyes fixed on the car and realizing I was almost in an accident, I let my breath out between clinched teeth and said some words that could not qualify as a prayer of gratitude.

The driver of the SUV shook her fist and waved her arms at me as if I was sitting there in traffic, stopped behind dozens of other cars, just to purposefully and personally cause her a delay. Although I am always happy to see another Italian individual waving arms in wild gestures of self-expression (a trait we Italian people are famous for—with good reason), I was pretty sure this lady wasn't attempting to relate to me from an ethnic identity corner.

My own Italian-Irish temper began to infuse my thought patterns as I grew more annoyed with her hand signals and horn honking. I've seen, and been the victim of, out of control road raging. I've learned there is nothing I can do to make it better, but tons of stuff I can do to make it worse. I sat in my car, kept my eyes on the cars in front of me, controlled my own hands (prone to return gesture engagement) and prayed for temper control. I also asked God for a temporary case of lockjaw if she got out of her car and came toward me.

I prayed out loud, "Lord, please intervene and use something, anything, to return me to my previously serene mindset."

As the traffic crawled forward, the driver in the SUV decided we weren't moving fast enough and took matters into her hands. She swung around my right back bumper, missing it by inches, and put her foot down hard on the accelerator of her vehicle as she traveled the right turn lane for the entire length of one-half block. When she passed me, she showed me the lovely manicure she had on only one finger of her left hand and shouted something I'm glad I couldn't hear. As she sped past, I saw a sign in her back window. It read, "Please drive with care—baby on board."

I burst out laughing and thanked God for His impeccable comic relief timing. I also petitioned Him to keep me from thinking, "Baby on board indeed—behind the wheel." Okay, I admit I did think that.

As I made my way to my meeting, I continued thanking God that even in the most irritating situations, if I turn to Him in prayer for deliverance, He will show up without fail. He has my backside and, in this case, my car's backside. He chose to use something that can usually pull me out of a situation where I can make things worse. He used His glorious Holy Humor.

Today's Prayer

Lord, please show me where I can intentionally walk today with the idea that taking offense when others are unkind can never be in anyone's best interest. Help me to thank you as I remember you are the great physician who proves that laughter is indeed the best medicine.

Blow Holy Spirit

Breathe on me sweet song from above,
in the mirror of His great, limitless love.
Help me stand still, yielding only to you,
as I intentionally always say thank you.

Bending my will through sighs of release,
help me live, resting in unruffled peace.
The door opens with soft, fragrant warm air,
you have called me to trust and meet you there.

Let me sit and watch all hurry go by,
drinking in your endless spiritual sky.
Help me remember you are my true home,
capturing thoughts that rumble and roam.

So, breathe on me sweet song from above,
in the mirror of His great, limitless love.
Help me stand still in deep gratitude,
whether with others or in blessed solitude.

Part Two

Surrender Salad

While learning about meal preparation, I found salad to be my favorite place to create a variety of diverse dishes. Even as a child, I learned it is important to surrender my preconceived notions of what a salad may look like. That often proves to be the better plan by far.

When I used to think of surrender, it was sometimes through the lens of giving up. Now, I prefer to think of it as giving over—my will, my own ideas, and my attachment to what I am sure will work best.

Just as salad has a variety of elements and can look differently in different situations, so it is with surrender. When I examine my more than seventy years on earth, I am amazed at the assorted elements I have surrendered in a variety of circumstances and been better for doing that.

In this human form, God does not ask me to submit to oppression, and that is not His way. Instead, He offers me opportunities to give Him the control which can happen in an assortment of parts and pieces.

Powerless Ain't Popular

Sometimes there are no answers

When my younger sister, and best friend, was diagnosed with terminal cancer in late 2023, I went through an array of mental gymnastics. I felt we were owed an answer to what caused this. How did Mary get this death sentence? Who, or what, was responsible?

I felt all the emotions that go with loss, death and dying. I was sad, hurt, in denial, and trying to make deals with God. If I am honest, I was angry. In my anger, I talked to anyone who would listen to my insistence that there had to be an answer. Someone had to pay.

One day as my husband and I had coffee with some friends, I posed this question once again. What caused this? One of the gentlemen was, himself, living with terminal cancer. His voice was soft as he asked several questions in response to my question.

"What would you do with that information? How can it help with the journey you are about to undertake with Mary? Asking for an explanation is part of your new journey and it is one way you may feel you have control. But what will you do with the information right now? How will it help your sister at this point?" he asked.

I was speechless as my mind turned the words over and sought to bring some light into the excruciatingly heavy darkness. I had no answer and just shook my head as the truth of his words made a pathway into my reluctant heart.

After our meeting with those dear friends, I began to realize that my quest for answers was fueled by the anger that spoke to the unfairness of the situation we now found ourselves staring in the face.

I spent many days thinking about my friend's calm response that reflected his acceptance of his condition after probably spending time trying to find a way to control what was going on with him. I realized that to be angry about this was part of the path we now walked. But his words were what helped me to release an emotion that would not help the situation and in fact could render me unable to step into the role of caregiver for one of my precious lifelong companions.

Being freed from the energy-depleting anger was a gift given to me by a friend who recognized I would need to be able to have a clear head in the days ahead. I never got a chance to thank that friend, because he too lost his battle with cancer a few short months after Mary's passing.

But I have told his wife how submitting to the reality of the situation was a strength builder that came in handy during the last two months of Mary's life. Without the truths gently spoken by her husband, the situation would have been complicated by my trying to control and force an answer that would then, and now, likely never come.

We live in a world where humans are taught that we have control over our lives and situations. In fact, however, we do not have control over many, and perhaps most, things. This myth of control is not a posture that sells commodities. Instead, it entices us to perform at higher levels than may be healthy.

Sometimes, there are no answers. Perhaps releasing my entitlement to know everything, a false sense of control, was a lesson in living in peace with no answers to some questions as I rely upon the One who does know. I thank my friend who in his own pain and struggle was kind, and brave, enough to speak a truth I needed. I praise God for the lesson of surrendering my anger because of words from a wise man who helped me prepare to navigate the sacred road of walking Mary home.

Today's Prayer

Father God, help me be willing to see beyond the moment or situation into what I might really be saying if I insist on control while overlooking the One I claim to be my guide in life.

Nailed It

Releasing the past, embracing His peace

There it was again, a memory I thought I had left behind twenty plus years ago. But in the early hours of a cold Colorado morning, I awoke with this as a bookmarked entry on my mind's playlist. Was it a dream? Did the memory awaken me? Was I already awake when it surfaced? It made no difference. There it was.

The thought of leaving my warm bed was not attractive in the least. Still, I decided a hot cup of herbal tea and a few minutes in prayer would help me regain my slumber. I padded out to the kitchen in my fuzzy panda slippers and chenille robe to put the kettle on.

As I sat in the dark, sipping the hot liquid, snuggling in my fleece blanket and favorite chair, I was hit by waves of guilt. The haunting infraction replayed without missing a single, unpleasant, vivid detail. I shook my head back and forth, trying to clear the image of directing anger and frustration at a loved one two decades ago.

"What am I doing back here, Lord? Why are you punishing me? I've tried to make up for this. I've apologized to you, to the one I hurt and have felt forgiveness from both. Why am I still standing on the guilt meter about something I cannot change?"

The room was silent...and cold. I waited.

The memory of the incident replayed. The hurt on my loved one's face seared my conscience and pierced my heart.

"Lord, I'm so sorry. Please forgive me. Will I live forever with this awful memory of terrible behavior fed by an unleashed temper and untamed tongue?" Tears of shame crawled down my cheeks, then progressed to a steady stream in a matter of seconds.

"Father God. Please forgive me."

On the flat-screen of my brain, a New Testament verse appeared, edging out the glaring transgression. "Their sins and lawless acts I will remember no more" (Hebrews 10:17 NIV).

I felt God was saying, "I have forgiven you child." His truth filled my heart and ears as we sat together in a once familiar room, now made foreign as regret framed the dark, shadow-less space.

"Then why is it still here? Why tonight? What must I do to remove it? Please Lord, what must I do?" I wailed.

There is nothing more valuable than the Scriptures at any time, but especially when we are in pain. My mind focused on another memorized verse. "Be kind and compassionate to one another, forgiving each other, just as in Christ God forgave you" (Ephesians 4:32 NIV).

I sat stunned as I realized God was saying that in this case, I was the "one another." I needed to be compassionate with myself and forgive the person I continued to condemn—me. I had been assured repeatedly of God's love and forgiveness. I also had been granted forgiveness from my loved one. Yet, I still clung to my guilt, shame, and human fallibility with a death grip.

Billions upon billions of sins were nailed to the cross at Calvary. And it never occurred to me, until that moment, my lack of forgiveness for myself was in essence un-nailing of sin that was covered by His precious blood. Yes, even this sin had been borne by our Savior on that rough wood, in His wounded body, so that I would not be rendered sleepless, immobile and at risk for use and abuse by my own thoughts. My revisiting this event and resisting the healing balm of Christ's sacrifice amounted to showing ingratitude for that sacrifice.

I closed my eyes and sipped the now tepid tea. I handed my pain, my past, my guilt, and my unforgiving heart up to the Lord to be placed where they belonged. Even when my unconscious mind unleashes memories of wrong-doing on my part, I can choose to see a nail driven through them like billions of other sins. My tears dried as I gathered my blanket around me and felt Christ's arms enfold me.

After a few minutes, I walked back to my bed and crawled in with my fleece blanket still wrapped around me like God's sweet truth. There is no need to hold onto guilt. There is no need to continue letting memories of a past and painful time consume me to the point of distress. I was forgiven at my first confession decades ago. And Jesus took that sin to the cross with innumerable others over two thousand years ago; and there it was nailed.

Today's Prayer

Lord, forgive me for cheapening your grace by continuously beating myself or others up for past offenses, as I learn to surrender my past infractions into the sea of your forgiveness.

Keeping My Beak in My Own Business
What? I do not have all the answers?

My husband, Keith, and I could not help laughing at the red-headed finch as he tried to eat out of a hummingbird feeder. We were at our kitchen table watching the hummingbirds come and go as they enjoyed their breakfast. Their delicate balance of swiftly flapping wings and taking sustenance has always been a delightful way to start our day. This delicate dance was in stark contrast to the finch who despite his comical contortions, including standing on his head, was unable to extract food from the tiny spout.

"What in the world has possessed that bird to think he can get his large, blunt beak into that little hole that's meant for a long, needle-like beak?" It just seemed preposterous to me that with his own feeder full of bird seed meant for him and the other larger birds in our yard, he would waste his time and energy trying to eat in what seemed to be an impossible situation.

Long after Keith left the breakfast table, I remained glued to the scene of what I considered silly, albeit, entertaining. The finch was less than thirty feet from a feeder designed for him to have his fill of bird food. Yet, here he was hopping from one resting shelf to the other, poking his beak into the too-tiny holes and coming up empty, without exception. Was he just being nosy? Did he think he needed to know what was going on with something that had nothing to do with him? Was he participating in the mindset of "the food's always sweeter on the other side of the yard?"

As is God's way sometimes, I can find myself in a classroom designed to teach me a lesson by using creatures outside the human variety. I am the first to admit, I would not voluntarily register for such instruction on God's syllabus. But if I pay attention, I can find myself sitting, learning, and understanding lessons that were not apparent to me through other means.

I watched as the finch did everything he could to have what another bird had, while completely ignoring what had been designed and supplied just for him. His frustration was evidenced in his loud squawking and increasing pace of hopping from one shelf to the next. He would have what his fellow birds had, no matter what the cost. This would happen even if it meant he would go hungry while the other large birds sucked down all the bird seed meant for him too. He had no concern, apparently, that he appeared insane in his unsuccessful feeding frenzy.

Whoa, wait a minute here. This was one of those moments when I think that although I love the book of life, the actual lab can be a little unappealing. I have been known to try and avoid that part of the class altogether.

Wasn't I just last week trying to fit into a situation where I did not belong? Wasn't it me whose beak, not too long ago, had been stuck into something that was none of my business? How many times have I envied another for the gifts given to them and how God has provided in their direction, while blatantly ignoring what He has given to and provided for me? Had I really forgotten the lessons learned, (the hard way) of being spiritually hungry due to my own refusal to take from the hand that always knows what I need? I cannot count the times I have tried to force solutions that I really believed were the right ones for me, or another, just to find I was performing insane and unproductive (even harmful) antics in my stubborn persistence.

Oh my, here before me was laboratory evidence of the book of life's great lessons. I was amazed, amused, and very humbled to think I was so quick to judge this bird for his attempts to secure food in a way not meant for him, when all along God was trying to show me what happens when I try to force solutions to satisfy my own needs and wants.

Knowing how much God loves me, I laughed out loud. What a brilliant and gentle teacher. His lessons are never condemning. He does not teach by demeaning. But rather, He finds ways to demonstrate what might be going on and what I might want to look at to make my walk with Him richer and my human life more peaceful and fulfilled.

I made another cup of tea and sat to watch as the hummingbirds fed and the red-headed finch moved on to his own feeder. I guess he finally figured out he had no business sticking his beak into something that was not his business, was not meant for him and certainly would never bring a yield for his best interests. And as I ran my finger around the rim of my cup, I mused that the red-headed finch was not the only one that day who learned to keep his beak in his own business.

Today's Prayer

Father God, please make me willing to surrender my ego that gets in the way of the humility which brings your peace.

The Adventures of Stick Woman

Insisting on steering the boat, my way

"Well, would you look at that?" I said while trying to call my husband's attention to a comical scene playing out in the rushing waters of the Uncompahgre River. One of our favorite afternoon walks is on the banks of this river that runs from the nearby San Juan Mountains. In the early spring, the river rises and rushes as it absorbs the snow melt from high peaks just south of our little town.

On this afternoon, we were enjoying the crisp, clean air and checking the water for clarity and speed, in an effort for Keith to assess his fishing prospects. It was not the water itself that provided entertainment. It was a small stick that had fallen from a nearby tree and was floating a few feet from shore. Despite the river's attempt to wash the stick downstream, the stubborn piece of wood resisted. Instead, it fought its way against the current to go in a direction that was opposite of normal flow. It moved head first into the eddies around rocks that produced unsafe travel.

I could not believe the stick's tenacity as it was battered against rocks and caught in swirling water that made its chosen voyage close to impossible. Still, the stick tried forcing its way and insisting on its own course. I watched this for a good bit of time and then shook my head at the futility of such activity.

I turned my attention from the stick's struggles and rested my eyes on the nearby mountains. I drank in the serenity provided by just sitting with my guy and watching the world flow by.

This peaceful pause in the day was interrupted when my thoughts turned once again to an unpleasant situation I had no control over. I just knew if I kept trying harder to explain my side, I could convince another person of my worth and the validity of my point of view.

Now, I am old enough to know that we cannot make others see things our way, no matter how hard we might plead our case. I felt as battered and bruised as the stick. I even sighed and said, "Yeah, I know the journey my wee wooden friend."

Then I burst out laughing. I realized I was amused by the battle of the stick, but not seeing I was engaging in the same type of fruitless maneuvers to orchestrate an outcome that was likely not going to come about. I pronounced myself a kindred soul and thought, "I am a human stick woman."

Keith thought I was still laughing at the stick's antics until I admitted that I had seen a new way of looking at an old, unhealthy situation. I told him that just like the stick, I was allowing myself to be battered, bruised and thrown about on a course that was proving all but impossible to travail. Because we had discussed the situation at length, we both chose not to go back over the details.

Allowing this truth to wash over me, my fretting ended almost immediately. I knew that to go against the tide in this case was only going to result in more harm and probably not affect the outcome I desired. All my explaining and attempts at reasoning were not going to be useful.

Because lunchtime was near, we reluctantly left our little respite site and headed for nourishment. Before we walked more than a few yards, I turned to see the stick finally yielding to the gentle pull of the mighty river as it floated gracefully, peacefully, and serenely downstream. "Hmm, well would you look at that?"

Today's Prayer

Lord, please make me willing to watch all around me as you supply the answers to questions, some of which I've not even asked yet.

The Heavenly Hoover

Releasing dust into the air

"I am so tired of wind. What purpose does it really serve anyway?" I grumbled as I made a cup of black tea and sat by a window where I could see the trees and bushes dancing with their invisible partner. Even though windy spring days are common in Colorado, I can be caught off guard and fall into complaining about the inconvenience and, what I consider, discomfort.

I wanted to go outside for a walk that morning, but the wind kept me inside because it plays havoc with my ears and sinuses. Instead of walking, I chose to sit by the window, sip the tea, and complain to God that this weather element He created seemed a little useless, in my opinion. I persisted in explaining that physical exercise is one way I keep my assigned temple healthy. The wind continued to blow. I continued to offer my logical arguments against the squall outside my window.

My annoyance was short-lived as my attention was captured by a small tree not far from the window where I sat. It was engaged in battle with the fast air movement. With each wind burst, dead leaves (remnants of the previous year's foliage) were released. It was as if the wind was a natural vacuum cleaner, removing debris from the branches. As the tree let go of what was no longer of use, it appeared to stand taller and straighter, relieved of unnecessary baggage. I imagined Mother Nature in her multi-pocketed apron pushing an invisible upright Hoover sweeper around each tree branch.

I was hypnotized by the pattern of air gusts met by branch resistance and then the relaxation of the branches as the wind force lessened periodically. I became lulled out of my discontentment and focused on a scene playing out in front of me. When the tree was almost entirely free of dry lifeless leaves, I thought it would no longer be engaged in the war with the wind. But as I squinted and peered closer, it appeared there was a small branch determined to hang onto one dead leaf, no matter the cost and even if the branch broke under the pressure exerted by the air stream.

It didn't take long to understand that if the branch would relinquish its grip on the dead leaf, it would no longer be in this uncomfortable and dangerous struggle. Now surely the branch does not have the cognitive ability to surrender that which is dead and no longer serving it. But what about me?

God in His wise and patient teaching used a beautiful natural illustration to gently show me that, in my own life, I can sometimes hold onto elements that are not producing any positive good in my life. I closed my eyes in prayer and thanked God for this sweet lesson in His vast classroom.

I knew God was giving me an exercise in health that was valuable beyond that outdoor walk I was unhappy about missing. As I sat quietly listening to the wind, I asked God if there were things I needed to release for my mental and spiritual health. I asked Him to show me where there were areas I needed to forgive. Perhaps I needed to ask forgiveness or reach out to a friend I may have hurt. I asked Him to help me inventory where my resentments and entitlements lay in the face of so much loss and denial of what I wanted, especially in the last year and a half. I truly wanted to know what God was trying to sweep away.

Before leaving my chair by the window, I looked at the ground beneath the tree and noticed a brown, dead leaf. When I looked up to the little tree branch, I saw it was no longer resisting the wind. It was straight, and the wind was blowing around, but not at, it. I was thrilled to see the emergence of a new, tender, baby leaf in place of the dead one.

"I see Lord. Looks like I may need to let go of some useless matter in my own life, to make room for new growth in You, huh? Okay, nice one," I said. After two deep sighs, I smiled and decided to make another cup of tea.

Now, I cannot honestly say I welcome the windy days in my little western Colorado community with open arms, for reasons I mentioned at the start of this story. But I can say that I understand all things in God's creation can be seen through the lenses of learning, growing and maybe even releasing. I am beginning to understand more deeply that nothing in God's created universe is without use. And sometimes, He just asks that I embrace a needed cleansing for spiritual fitness.

Today's Prayer

Father God, may I surrender my heart, soul, and mind to your daily removal of those things holding me back from my growth journey in you.

What about the Prodigal's Mom?
A study in silent brokenness

Today, our children are faced with greater dangers than ever before in America's history. A wrong decision or choice can have a disastrous outcome. No matter how we raise them, kids can make unhealthy choices, and parents can feel helpless in the face of those choices. I have learned that in those times, it is only God we can turn to for comfort. This truth is especially evident when answers we seek are slow to come, or if they do not come at all.

This helplessness is demonstrated in the Biblical story of the prodigal son. It is about a faithful father who waits for the return of a son gone off to squander his inheritance, leaving dad and a brother to run the family farm (Luke 15:11-32). Here we read about people thrown into turmoil, awaiting return of one who turned his back on what most people consider the jewel of our existence—family.

The parable focuses on the father, the prodigal, and the brother. Recently, however, I had occasion to consider events from the lens of the wayward child's mother. Although she does not appear in the text, I found myself wondering about her feelings and thoughts in an uncertain and, no doubt, heartbreaking time.

A few weeks prior to writing this piece, I was in an emergency room holding the hand of a friend experiencing disbelief and fear because her son drove while intoxicated and had an accident. This was not the first time. Through sobs of frustration, she pronounced herself the parent of a modern-day prodigal. We sat in silence, awaiting audience with an ER physician, and I mentally revisited that parable. My focus drifted from the father and son to the mother in that family. I pondered what was in the heart of that disappointed, saddened, and frightened mother long ago. While trying to comfort my friend and work through my own thoughts and feelings, many questions arose.

What about the Prodigal's Mom

What about the mom of the prodigal son?
Did she wonder where her baby had gone?
Was she worried, frightened, blaming herself?
Did she seek him, or put her heart on a shelf?

Were her nights sleepless as she tossed and turned?
Was she longing for what had been learned?
Did she fight and hold on, not letting go?
But heard the words, "He is a man now, you know."

Did she go to the gate on her own some days?
Did her tears blot out the sun's warming rays?
Did she shout and ask, "Where is my God?"
Did she try to know the roads her son trod?

Did she go to her man for answers she sought?
Then wept and moaned when answers came not?
Did she see others' children as their special joy?
And then secretly grieve the loss of HER boy?

Did she seek counselors to find none around?
Then pound her fists on unyielding ground?
Was her daily life on hold or at bay?
Did she want to die until that one day?

When she looked to heaven and could see,
God reaching, weeping, "Come, talk to me."

Today's Prayer

Lord, when my head is bowed in broken loneliness, please help me to look up and see I am never alone, and You weep with me.

Part Three

The Main Course

Without doubt, for me, the main course of any meal is a source of great joy. To savor the actual fruits of the labor that go into preparation and presentation, fills me with giddy delight. Sometimes the meal is light and sometimes heavy, depending upon the day, the situation, and my needs.

I have found this to be true of my life also. As I walk through my seventh decade, I am finding the application of the lessons I have learned along the way to be the bulk of my sustenance in good times and not so good times. God's great classroom and gentle, patient teaching methods offer me opportunities to reflect upon, and apply, His truths. And when I am filled with the goodness of His guidance and can look back to what I have learned, hopefully, I can share that to help others. That is the beauty of resting in the main course of life.

On the Other Hand
And there is always another hand

One of my favorite pastimes is going to musical theater productions. And one of my favorite musical theater productions was, and still is, "Fiddler on the Roof." The reason for this is not only great singing and dancing but the message sent by the main character, Tevye.

We meet this man in the complex world of an adult navigating the difficult terrain of humanity. Like all of us, he must make choices almost daily as to what is right or wrong for the good of himself, his family, and his community.

Tevye calls upon his family values, education, culture, religion, and mostly "tradition" to make his way through the cumbersome paths presented in everyday life. And even though these things play a major role in how he conducts his life, he is a critical thinker. Why? Because, in most of Tevye's predicaments, we witness him suspending his judgment based in the factors above and saying, "But, on the other hand."

That, in a nutshell, is the basis for my education in a Jesuit University. The Jesuits pride themselves not so much on teaching what to think but how to think. That requires weighing options and looking for solutions to problems through various lenses. In other words, "On the other hand."

This idea is supported by the Apostle Paul when he speaks to a Greek audience. Here is how it rolls out: Paul stood in the middle of the Areopagus, (a hilltop in ancient

Greece where philosophers came to debate) and said, "For as I was walking along, I saw your many shrines. And one of your altars had this inscription on it: 'To an Unknown God.' This God, whom you worship without knowing, is the one I'm telling you about." (Acts 17:23 NLT).

Please note that Paul acknowledges the beliefs, education, and traditions of these men without dismissing or disrespecting them. He knows that to gain an audience, he must first offer dignity to his listeners by not setting them up to be wrong and himself to be right. After letting them know he has heard and observed their beliefs, he introduces another way of seeing God by presenting the Gospel of Jesus Christ. It is equivalent to saying, "But, on the other hand."

We are not told if Paul was able to lead these gentlemen to faith in Christ. But I think it is a safe bet he had a lot better chance of introducing the Gospel by starting out validating them rather than rejecting or setting aside their beliefs and traditions.

Is there a lesson for us here? Is there a demonstration of entering into a dialogue that may lead to conversations instead of conflict? Yes, I think there is. And I believe it is not just about belief systems. I think this type of entrance into community discussions can be used in almost any conflict situation.

Perhaps I am just speaking from my own training in critical thinking and persuasion. But no matter how right I think I am, I must remember there is always more to be learned by listening to others. I believe there is always cause to say, "But, on the other hand."

Today's Prayer

Father God, when I am tempted to tell others that I know something and they do not, help me to apply the same tact and diplomacy as St. Paul by affirming them and inviting them into dialogue.

Citizens of the World

A lesson from Estonia

What was this woman, who lived halfway across the world from me, trying to say? I could not speak her language (Estonian) and she could speak only a few words of mine (English). By many people's standards, we could not communicate. But she seemed to think we could understand one another as she took my hand and placed it on various pieces of fiber art she had created.

My husband and I were with a tour group as part of our trip to the Baltic Sea, where we visited several countries. In each place we were delighted to eat the food, hear the history and try, even in a limited amount of time, to soak up what we could of the culture.

Estonia's history is full of stories of occupation, loss and violence perpetrated by actions by other countries, particularly Russia. Despite the scars, the people are proud of their resilience and that they eventually gained independence and maintained their own identity through language, music, architecture, and fine art.

As we toured one of the houses (manors) with its expansive grounds, we heard about the owners of the property. They were forced to leave during the Russian siege in the 1940s. One of the owners returned to her home around 1991, when Estonia became independent of Russia.

We didn't see the owner until the end of our house tour. When we did meet her, she was seated at her loom and weaving a blanket. Questions were asked and answered through an interpreter for several minutes. Then most of the tourists moved outside to view the sprawling manor grounds.

I stayed back, captivated by her handiwork. As a knitter and embroidery enthusiast, I was riveted to the work before me. She noticed my interest and came to join me. As others looked at the trees and nearby buildings, I walked from table to table admiring embroidered pieces, handmade lace and many woven lap robes made from fox fur and linen strips.

We were silent until she took my hand and guided me to an oil painting of a woman, a man, a young boy, and small girl. She put her hands to her chest and said, "Before."

"You?" I asked.

She smiled, nodded, pointed to the tiny girl and whispered, "Before."

My eyes lingered on her as she gazed upon the painting. She seemed unaware that I was searching her face and eyes. I wanted to know what she felt. Was she sad, angry, resentful, defeated, or regretful? No, none of those were in her sweet, calm countenance. Instead, I soaked in the presence of acceptance, loving memories and peace. I sensed that she treasured the past but did not live there, neither in the joy nor pain. Her life was here, and now. I believe that is what she was trying to tell me.

She noticed me looking at her and blushed. Then she motioned for me to join her at a large table where she opened a book and handed me a pen. "Sign please?"

I wrote my name, where I live and a blessing. We smiled, held hands, and shared a moment of heart-to-heart connection. She handed me an apple resting in a bowl containing two pieces of fruit. I thought it must have been from one of her trees. She beamed as she offered this treasure. I gratefully accepted it, as if it was fine gold. To me it was.

We couldn't speak the same language or discuss anything that the world might consider relevant. But in those few moments of shared artistic inspiration and expression, I was allowed into her world—the past and the present. We were in a space void of politics, religion, language, or nationality. And it was more than okay with us.

As our tour bus left the grounds, I looked back to see her on the front porch and waving. I waved back and clutched the apple to my breast wondering how many people come on this tour each year, look at the obvious but don't spend time trying to find out who she was and is. I am grateful God granted us just the briefest moment of connection because we share a mutual love of fiber arts. I leaned back in my seat and rested in the knowledge that, through smiling eyes, an extra moment of lingering and the human touch, we recognized each other as citizens of the world.

Today's Prayer

Lord, please help me daily to apply the lessons you have taught me about your children belonging to each other, whether we are in different countries, cultures, and religions.

Cross and Shield
Who really fights the battle?

Ten years ago, Keith bought me a piece of jewelry that I wear often. It is a white abalone shield with a cross carved out in the middle. We were going through a particularly volatile time in our lives for many reasons. Each day I would get up and say, "I am weary, Lord. I just cannot keep fighting these battles and still do the work you have called me to do as a dance minister and author. I am so weary."

During different parts of the journey, I took out the abalone pendant and held it close. I would envision myself standing under, and clinging to, the bloodstained cross of Christ. I imagined struggling to hold His shield of protection in front of me as a means of deflecting the external unpleasantness. It became quite heavy, and I would tell God at the end of the day how weary I was of it all.

I really believed it was up to me to do the work of holding the shield in front of me while physically leaning into the cross for the stability needed to keep standing. I had been in several conversations where I was defending myself from words of others. In my efforts, I became overwhelmed to the point of becoming defensive and sometimes lashing out from a heart full of resentment and self-righteousness. After all, I held the shield, didn't I?

Then one day while doing my devotions, and holding my necklace, God clearly reminded me of similar times when, by not allowing Him to hold the shield for me, I had made things worse. I sat quietly and remembered, in detail, how letting God be my defender always turned out to be the right step.

"Am I trying to fight my own battles again, Lord?" I asked.

"Are you not my child? I need you to understand that the shield and cross are symbols that assure you I am always your protection. And I loved and do love you enough to go to the cross. All I ask is that you hand Me those lies that you are choosing to believe about who runs the show here. Those lies are taking your energy and hardening your heart."

I removed my blinders and saw that my defensiveness was based in the fact that I believed it was up to me to bring people to a point of seeing me in a more favorable light, even if it meant a heated battle. It had also become almost an obsession to make others see things my way.

I reflected upon the fact that the cross bore the weight of my past failures and temptations to retaliate. I saw, not for the first time, that God was asking me to inventory my own attitudes and heart; then guard my heart and trust fully in Him.

This verse had shown up in my devotional materials off and on for several weeks. "Above all else, guard your heart, for everything you do flows from it." (Proverbs 4:23 NIV). The word *guard* took on a whole new meaning as it became clearer every day that I needed to wear that cross and shield as a reminder that the One who protects me was/is doing the battle. Believing otherwise was to expose my heart and mind to an unguarded, dangerous path.

Today I still wrestle with unkindness and untruth all around me. Who doesn't in this world? But now I more fully accept the truth of the cross and hand the shield to the only one who truly can protect me. He is able and willing to defend me, even from the condemnations of my own voice and heart that can lead to me hurting myself or others.

Today's Prayer

Father God, please help me to be willing to intentionally move under your protection instead of feeling the need to do battles that are not mine to fight.

Got Vasa?

Burdens that can sink me

"That is just ridiculous. What an idiotic thing to do," the man, standing next to me, muttered to his companion. He was referring to the construction of a ship called Vasa (pronounced Va:sa, with an accent on the last syllable). It is housed in the Vasa Museum in the Royal National City Park in Stockholm, Sweden. My husband and I toured this while visiting that great Scandinavian city.

Our guide, as we toured the museum, told us Vasa is the legendary ship built by the King of Sweden in 1626–1627. It was commissioned as a symbol of the King's military ambition and designed to be a powerful war vessel armed with tons of bronze cannons. The Swedish King, Gustavus Adolphus, used most of the country's resources to establish a powerful military presence in his campaign to occupy countries in the Baltics and defeat Poland-Lithuania during a conflict he initiated in 1621.

Formidable as she was, and no doubt ready to prove her superiority in battle, Vasa was unable to make it farther than 1,400 yards out of the harbor on her maiden voyage in August, 1628. Due to instability caused by unbalanced weight from heavy battle equipment in the upper portion of her hull, she sank moments after leaving port. Despite warnings, the King proceeded with the launch that resulted in destruction of the vessel and loss of lives. The ship was salvaged and restored as closely as possible to its original form in 1961.

Today it sits in a museum designed to house this piece of Swedish history.

Spending time listening to the story and gazing at the mammoth ship, I couldn't help but remember times when I too had figuratively left port loaded up for battle. My life was defined by conflicts that I felt I had to win and foes I felt I had to conquer. I could not rest unless I won arguments, most of which I found a way to start. That has changed significantly as I have studied at the knee of the Prince of Peace.

No one can deny that, in 2025, there is no shortage of opportunities to engage in conflict. Particularly in recent times. As events in our country/world have escalated in violence, division, uncertainty, and fear, I have felt increasingly more tempted to take control of the uncontrollable elements around me. That is when God reminds me, I have choices about how I journey through this world.

As Keith and I have traveled this world, learned from her people, listened to the stories and histories of others, I am enriched by what God teaches. I do not believe He sends lessons to shame or blame. I believe He wants me to release the burdens that can keep me from doing the work He has assigned for me. He also expects me to rest in the lessons as I enjoy this main course time in my life.

Because I believe in the value of spiritual inventory, I've begun to wake up each day, look in the mirror and ask, "Got Vasa today? Or is there another way to sail the seas of uncertainty, division and sometimes fear?" It really is a personal choice. I can either return to what I once was or remember the hard lessons that have brought me into a different way of thinking and interacting with others.

I know I cannot do this by my own power. Trying to do so adds frustration to the sometimes complicated atmosphere of my human existence. When it comes to releasing those heavy cannons designed for battle and destruction that keep me from enjoying smooth sailing, I have found it is simply a matter of being willing to ask for help.

Today's Prayer

Lord, I praise you for the creative ways you find to remind me where I have been and what lessons I have learned. I ask you to keep reminding me to apply those lessons so I can make good choices, the right choices, on a regular basis.

Road Work Ahead
One of life's realities

Every Wednesday is date day at our house. Keith and I spend our midweek, whether winter or summer, exploring areas around us in search of nature's beautiful bounty. There is no shortage of opportunity to find God's handiwork and hear His voice in the Rocky Mountains of Colorado.

On one of our date day adventures, we found ourselves stopped on the road due to construction. While we waited for traffic to clear, I saw we were parked by a sign that said, "Road Work Ahead." In viewing the work area, it appeared there would be some tough going to reach our destination. Although most of our trip so far had been smooth and free of difficulties, this part appeared to be more challenging.

We discussed the option of taking an alternate route by turning around to avoid inconvenience and difficulty, or continuing along the construction route. As I stared at the sign off and on for the twenty minutes we were parked by it, I felt that through these three words, on this orange diamond-shaped sign, God was speaking to me.

You see, in recent months I had entered a period of deep grieving at the loss of my younger (but much wiser) sister, Mary. She also was my best friend of seventy years. Some days are rocky and uncertain. Some days flow smoothly.

Many days, and indeed hours, I must choose whether to turn back from the hard and tumultuous terrain of grief work, or move forward and participate in the healing process. No one would blame me for choosing the former.

The sign on the road that day reminded me that all of life carries the message that there is "Road Work Ahead." There are rocky and smooth times. There are furrows, potholes, and unsteady soil. Can the announcement of impending work help me avoid difficulties and sometimes unpleasant surprises? No. But being aware that I am always on a road of working out life helps me sustain the trust needed to proceed. This is true throughout the diverse frameworks of humanity.

In my mind's eye, I see that sign each day. I take comfort in knowing that even though I am on this grief path, I am not alone. I've a lovely spouse and many friends and family who are walking it with me. I am grateful for that. Still, in the darkest hours, in the deep furrows of this grief, it is God and me. That is all that is needed. I trust Him to show me the way and when necessary to indicate, "detour ahead," when my human heart cannot sustain the load on the road. I rest in the knowledge that there will be times when He will post, "Road Closed." In all these, I defer to His guidance.

Date days are also for gleaning new knowledge and insights. For me, that little orange sign reminded me that I will always be on a road needing work, even in circumstances different from grief. That means I must be compassionate and patient with myself in my pilgrimage. It also means I should strive to be compassionate and patient with others. After all, I do not know what is going on in their lives. I believe that most people are also on a journey declaring, "Road Work Ahead."

Today's Prayer

Father God, the road each of us must travel is riddled with potholes, detours, uncertainty, and challenges. When I rest in the bulk of your blessings, I realize that, with you and when applying your truths, it is possible to travel all roads and engage in the work that you send.

On the Unkind Days
The surprise of soul connections

The line at my local coffee shop was not long, but the wait was because of a lengthy order being placed by a lady at the counter. She turned and looked at the man right in front of me and said, "I'm sorry, I'm buying for the office."

He responded by saying that was fine. But he leaned against the wall and seemed to be having trouble standing for a long time. If I were to guess, I would say he was in pain. Finally, he said I could take his place in line because he needed to sit down. I asked if I could get his coffee for him and he said that would not be necessary.

When the lady with the long order finished and paid, I turned to look for him. We made eye contact, and I motioned for him to come back to his original place. He declined and so I placed my order. As I began to purchase the drink, a voice to my left announced, "I will pay for hers." It was the man who was originally in line ahead of me.

My first inclination was to decline his offer. But his eyes were shining in a way that eyes do when we offer a gift. His smile was infectious and so, I resisted the choice to resist and said, "Thank you, Sir." Now his smile erupted to encompass his whole face. I was struck by the vibrant radiance coming from this man who moments ago looked to be grimacing in pain.

As I waited for my order, I thought of how, in my upbringing, I was taught to never accept a gift from a stranger.

After all, what might they want in return? What could be their motive? Yet in this gentle gesture, I realized he was telling me he appreciated that I had offered to help him.

As I left the shop, I turned to thank him again. He smiled and said, "You are welcome." It was the same radiant smile which told me this was about the soul, and his kind act was his thankful offering for my kind act. How differently could it have turned out if I stuck with my prideful old messages that mandate we do not, we must not...(fill in the blank).

That man and I were two people who had never met, and likely will not meet again. And in a time where suspecting others of different religions, politics, genders, or skin color is the norm, it was refreshing to just stand in a space with this stranger.

We live in a contentious, competitive world in this twenty-first century. Still, I always have the choice to resist negative, fear-based thoughts in favor of embracing the generosity of another. Sometimes, accepting kindness is an act of kindness, and this memory will warm my soul on those days that seem unkind.

Today's Prayer

Lord, you are the author of all goodness and kindness. Please make me aware of not only being kind but accepting kindness as I apply the lessons you have taught me for just such a time as this.

What Really Matters

Father gently blocks my immediate view,
of distractions from the season and day.
He draws my heart and soul to Him,
beckoning me to truths He will say.

In deep breaths of tranquility I find,
trust in the safety of Mother's arms.
Through ice-dotted, thickening fog,
the world is stripped of false charms.

As the dark comes and light departs,
I see an arena for lessons to learn.
Standing in search of my Teacher's voice,
I feel lifting of anxiety's cold burn.

Within the soft closing of hazy walls,
I release demands for solid reply.
I understand that here and now, at least,
there's no relevance in the question, "Why?"

𝒫𝒶𝓇𝓉 𝒻𝑜𝓊𝓇

The Delights of Dessert

As a child, dessert at dinner or lunch was seen as a reward for eating our meal. I did not always like what was on my plate but I ate it, mostly out of obedience, and to gain nourishment. This is true in my life as well. I am not always excited to embrace what is on my daily, weekly, or yearly agenda. Still, there are few experiences I have not learned from.

I have learned that when turning my life over to God and moving in the directions he prescribes, it is a matter of practicing obedience. One example is when called by God, in my forties, to enter the world of competitive, performative dance, I all but laughed out loud. He put on my heart an urge so strong to learn this art form and use it for His glory that I put aside my reluctance, pride, and the ageist messages I told myself. I obeyed and have been blessed to enjoy many delightful desserts of obedience, as I am sure was His plan all along.

Stat Tapping

Putting off derailment with creativity

"Oh no," I wailed to my husband when I got the transcript analysis that indicated what classes I was to take to finish my Bachelor's Degree. There it was, the bad news and the very bad news. I was required to take at least one math class to complete the degree. I had a choice of college algebra or statistics. I had failed the former in my early college years. The idea of taking the latter fell like a heavy book dropped on a bare toe.

I was going to have to forego the lifelong dream of completing a college education. I was in my early fifties and convinced this old dog could not learn new tricks. I couldn't get math and math would never get me. The despair was palpable at the dinner table.

"Why don't you just go to a class of statistics and see if it is something you can get through. Talk to the professor and see what might help you," Keith said. Grumbling and growling, I agreed. Maybe Keith was right.

But when I brought the book home and the assignments from the first class, I fell into doom and gloom again. I wrote page after page of the formula for standard deviation. Keith came home to a kitchen table littered with failed attempts at making the formula work. I could not remember how to plug in the numbers.

My husband, a math whiz, sat down and began to show me how to find homes for the numbers in the formulaic contortions. As he repeated the formula over and over again, he put it to a rhythm (to this day he has never admitted doing that on purpose).

At this point I had been taking tap and Irish Step Dancing classes for several years, and I began to see a tap dance routine. As I got up and started tapping out the rhythm, it cemented itself into my memory. I saw that I could transfer the rhythm to the paper by remembering each part as a dance step.

On the first exam, one week later, I caught the eye of my instructor. I must have been fidgeting in my seat because he motioned me forward and asked if I needed a bathroom break. I blushed and told him I was just nervous. After returning to my seat, I completed the exam and asked for an audience with him following class.

I decided the best course of action was to come clean and tell him the story of finding a way to tap my statistical formulas. His face was a mixture of disbelief and amusement as he said he had been teaching for thirty years and had never heard of such an extreme method for working through math problems. He was silent for several minutes as I shifted from one foot to the other like a four-year-old who just got busted poking her sister in the eye on purpose.

Then he stood up from his desk and said, "Alright. I will grant you the request of continuing this unusual testing strategy with one condition. You are to sit in the back row where there is carpeted flooring, wear thick soled shoes and make no noise to tap your answers onto the paper."

I began thanking him like he had just handed me a winning lottery ticket. He put up his hand to silence me. "And if I catch you teaching this to anyone else or see students studying your feet during exams, you will not only fail this class, you will be expelled from this university."

"That's very fair of you, Sir. Thank you," I said.

He shook his head, grumbled something unintelligible and went back to grading papers. I left the room and went home to work on my next dance routine for stats class.

I not only passed the class but got the highest grade. I kept my word and taught no one else in that class about my dance secret. But several years after my own graduation, I did share it with another friend who had the same class, the same problems, the same instructor, and was a dancer. She later told me that one day he walked up to her after an exam, looked at her and said, "Padgett, huh?" She nodded. He gave her the same boundaries, and she went on to ace the class as well.

Some think dance is for entertainment, competitions, performances, and expression of artistic expertise. While this is true, I will always believe this art form launched me into the graduation line as I was allowed to use it to walk (tap) through and apply formulas.

Today's Prayer

Father God, please help me remember there are many ways to use creativity of the arts to reach the goals you have ordained.

Who Says You Can't?

Dismissing the world's definition of can

Have you ever been in a gathering of family or friends and felt yourself drawn to a stranger for reasons you cannot explain? Have you ever followed the desire to connect with that person? If you have, did you realize that it probably was God trying to give you a gift through their words, actions, or demeanor? Did you consider that it might just be God offering you the opportunity, through obedience to His voice, to gift another by sharing from your own experiences?

While attending a college alumni event several years ago, I spent most of the evening catching up with former classmates. As I moved through the crowd, I noticed there was one particular woman I felt a strong pull toward. I was pretty sure I didn't know her.

After about an hour, my curiosity got the better of me, and I inquired, "Have we met before?"

She said, "No. I have never been to one of these functions until tonight."

"My name is Laura Padgett," I said, while offering my hand in greeting.

"Yes, I know. My name is Marion. They tell me you are a dancer. Is that right?" She inquired.

I smiled, nodded my head, and admitted it was true. I had only been dancing for about ten years and teaching dance for three or four. In that time, this had become part of my personal identity.

She told me, "I love to dance too. I wanted to be a dancer once. When I was a little girl, my mother took me for ballet lessons. The dance teacher told her I would never be a dancer, and that my mother was wasting her money. The teacher said I was just too clumsy to dance. In many ways, that statement has stayed with me and affected me throughout my entire life."

When it appeared she had finished with her story, I didn't hesitate before saying, in a firm voice, "She was wrong. She was wrong, my friend. Dancing is in the heart, not the body. True, there are those who achieve great heights in dance. They are to be respected and applauded for their efforts. But the technical merit of any art takes a back seat to the true heart of an artist. And art, my dear, lives in the soul that feeds on the joy of art and not on accomplishments nor accolades that may or may not accompany those accomplishments."

I took a break to catch my breath. She smiled at me with her whole person. In her sparkling green eyes, I saw that I was giving this sweet soul information that was not new to her. We sat down to enjoy a glass of white wine and more conversation about dance, art, what it means to be a teacher and, for that matter, what it means to be a student.

She told me that for many years she believed the words of the ballet teacher. She felt clumsy and physically inept. But in recent times, she began to arise each morning, turn on some music, close her curtains and dance in joy and freedom right in her living room. She stated she just moves to the music and dances. As she beamed at me, I understood and shared her bliss. I identified with her victory.

"Yes, I know, dear sister. I know," I assured her.

On the way home, I remembered similar tales I have heard during my years as a dance instructor. These stories are why I love to teach adults. In some ways I think, as a teacher of those who have been told they cannot be taught, God uses me to spread the word that all gifts are from Him and all recipients are worthy to use and share His art forms. I want my students to dance with their hearts first. If their bodies catch up, that's fine. But the goal is to move and be moved from deep inside. I believe God wants us to use the arts and not allow the arts to use us.

I also thought about how many times I have been told I wasn't "good enough" to do something. I revisited and then released the pain authored by false prophets.

I think the Lord often sends angels, in human temples, to relay new messages. Or perhaps He sends them to reaffirm the ones he has already taught. If we are open, we can hear His truths in the words of a stranger or see His love in the eyes of someone during a first encounter. As I rejoiced in the chance (?) meeting with Marion, God took the opportunity to remind me what my course must always be when I am sharing the arts I love. He told me that, as a teacher and an artist, my first call is to honor His children by encouraging, guiding, helping, and sharing. It is important to always teach and encourage with the same positive care and patience He shows me every day. Outcome is not the issue. Process is the point.

Not everyone in this world will be a champion or professional in any discipline. That is of no matter to our Father because, in His eyes, we are all gold medalists. I live under the truth (and I suspect Marion does as well), that no matter what anyone says I can't do, I can confidently reply, "But, my Daddy says I can."

My prayer that night was one of gratitude for meeting Marion, hearing her story, and learning about her courageous journey to dance no matter who says she will never be a dancer. I thanked Him for the reminder that, first and foremost, I am to hold the hearts and souls of my students in tender care and love. I asked God to keep me open to His voice when He says, "Go and talk to this person. It's important." In obedience to His call, I can never go wrong in my plight as a student or teacher.

Before I fell into sleep that night, I petitioned the Great One for one more item. I asked if He could help Marion to someday get up, put on her music, dance with all her heart, and leave her curtains open.

Today's Prayer

Lord, help me to always remember to be grateful for the good gifts you give and to know that they were not given for me alone, but for the joy of others as well.

Lessons from Las Vegas

Not leaving Vegas in Vegas

We have all heard the saying, "What happens in Vegas, stays in Vegas," right? Well, not necessarily.

There are few places I honestly can say I dislike. And Las Vegas is one. It's not my cup of tea. This is just a personal preference, nothing more.

So, one competitive dance season, I was less than enthused when I learned our clogging team was going to Vegas for a national competition. Don't get me wrong. I love my teammates. These ladies are good friends and I've been blessed to dance with some of them, on and off, for almost twenty years. Truly I could be in no better company, no matter where my little dancing feet take me.

The few months prior to the competition were not as smooth as I would have liked. I pulled a hamstring months before and had a hard time catching up to the level of dance needed for such an event. It's rare I say that I am too old for something. But let's face it, friends, the calendar doesn't lie. Injuries are harder to recover from now days. Still, I practiced and trained and laid out a fortune for chiropractic care and massage. Did I mention how much I love these ladies?

When the big week arrived, I remember asking, "Lord, what am I doing here?" I wasn't sure I was up to it and didn't want to cost the team a medal they so richly deserved. At last, the final day came—hours before show time, and one of my teammates asked, "Laura, would you be my stage mom?"

This meant that I was agreeing to help a teammate out of one costume and into another, complete with all necessary accessories, hair adjustment, and makeup check. I was thrilled. Of course I would be there for her. I said to myself, "Oh, perhaps this is what I'm doing here. I'm here to help my friend."

Right before we were called to dance, our director gathered us in a circle and told us how proud she was of us, how we had worked hard, and she had nothing but confidence in us. I cried as she spoke and we clustered together, listening to the coach and holding each other up, figuratively and literally. I thought, "Oh, this is why I'm here—to be part of a group I admire and love, and to take the stage with my mates in what is likely my last national competition."

When we were on stage, the lights went up and the music started. The game was on. There was no worry about forgetting steps/patterns. I stopped feeling unworthy to stand on that stage because of age or injury. There was a belonging and the knowledge that I am part of something I love and people I love dearly. There truly is something stimulating about flood lights, house lights, and a room full of young and old alike (not just our families) rocking, clapping, and jumping around because we are dancing our little hearts and souls out for them.

When your peripheral vision shows young kids (competitors) cheering you on and hopping around, there is a joyful feeding of the soul that is inexplicable. I told myself, "Oh, this is why I'm here—to offer others the bliss of the dance that I feel every time I move."

There are so many blessings listed here, but perhaps one of the best ones came after our performance. A young, (maybe thirteen years old), beauty from Honduras came up to me and said, "Tu eres muy bonita, Señora (you are very beautiful). Cuantos años..." She stopped short of asking the question, which could be considered rude and disrespectful. "How old are you?"

I took her beautiful young hands in mine and said, "I am sixty-three years old, my dear. And I want to tell you that you can do this for the rest of your life if you take care of yourself, honor your body and never allow anyone to take your dreams. Ok?"

She smiled at me and said, "That is what my grandmother says."

"I am a grandmother too, my dear," I told her, "And we are always right."

She ran off with her friends, then turned to wave at me. I smiled and mouthed, "Good luck." I winked, and she winked back.

I looked up to thank God for all my dancing friends and experiences over the years and around the country. Dancers ran by me, stage moms and teachers issued orders, and my stomach growled in annoyance at being denied. I stood in the chaos, excitement and craziness saying out loud, "Oh, this is why I'm here—to encourage a young person to be her best, treat herself well, and hold onto her dreams. Thank you, Father."

It wouldn't be right if I didn't tell you we won a platinum award for that dance (one level above gold). I would be lying if I didn't tell you I had the time of my life with my mates (dancing and just hanging out). I won't insult you by trying to make you believe I'm not tickled to know, "there is a dance in this old dame yet." And I'm sure it's not hard for my readers to imagine I shall always treasure the conversation I had with a young dancer about age, dancing, and dreams. This all was the result of obeying the call to go to a place I do not like and be part of a team of ladies I love.

But most importantly, I want you to know that what this grateful little dancer learned in Vegas that summer, will not just stay in Vegas.

Today's Prayer

Father, please let me remember that I am here to help, to teach, to encourage and to be helped, to be taught, to be encouraged and to learn. Mostly I am here to learn and to then teach what you have taught me. Help me to always obey that call.

Why Community?

God's beautiful design called family

Throughout my thirty plus years of dancing I was often asked why I belonged to many different communities of dancers. The truth is my life would not have been nearly as rich had I missed the opportunity to make friends with different dancers, from different lands and in a variety of situations and locations.

I see dance as many things including, but not limited to, spiritual, physical, and mental exercise. So, for people who ask me why I love to dance so much, these elements are easily understood. But sometimes it is not as easily understood why I prefer to dance in community with other dancers, especially in the worship experience of sacred dance.

Although I have seen, and participated in, solo work as a dancer, I am most fulfilled when entering the sacred space created with others while moving prayers and worship. I am always keenly aware of the family-like atmosphere permeating the world of sacred dance. But the reason I crave, and am fed by, community has never been clearer to me than when I participated in a three-day event with the International Sacred Dance Guild (SDG) in Ottawa, Canada one summer.

We were women and men from many countries, a variety of states/provinces, all church denominations, all ages, all dance abilities and training, and different ethnic groups. How can a short time together create a lasting bond and a longing to be back together at the next SDG festival or event? By all logical laws this would measure as unlikely. But for the sacred dancer, there is a deep spiritual need to express meaning in movement. Along with eagerness to accept one another, it is not hard to see the formation of a foundation for life-long connection.

I cannot say there was one dance I enjoyed more than others. But I can say that in a park, on a cloudy Sunday morning in Ottawa, we did a movement piece that brought me into a deeper understanding of why dance within community is vital to the health of my soul.

Each dancer was given a long string of clear beads. As the music began, a group of dancers moved with their beads extended over their heads, in front of them, to their side, or dragging on the ground. We danced slowly around the circle at first and then invited others to join. We moved with the beaded strings, independent of one another, for only a short while. Then we each extended one end to another dancer. Through the rest of the piece we moved in, out, and among the newly created formation. We let go of and took up continuing connections with each other. In the middle of the dance my mind registered this profound truth.

Here was a pure definition of community and an explanation for need to be part of one. That is not expressed or understood by words, for me. It is seen by the heart, expressed through the eyes, felt in the touch of another, and fueled by the movement of souls that know, just know, we are all beings who belong to each other. This I believe is God's design for human harmony and community.

Today's Prayer

Lord, may I move in beauty and connection as I continue learning how to celebrate diversity and embrace sameness.

Some Gave All

An earthly father's gift

"He was a hero you know."

A stranger announced this while I sat at my father's grave in Ft. Logan National Cemetery. It was Memorial Day Weekend. She was moving from grave to grave, placing small American flags in front of each headstone.

"Was he?" I asked.

She put a flag at my dad's headstone, and then turned to face me.

"Why, yes. All these men and women were heroes." She swept an arm around the immediate vicinity.

"They paid a high price for our freedom. Some paid with their physical and mental health; and some with their lives. We must never forget nor dishonor their sacrifices, nor that of their families," she said as she resumed her journey.

I stared at my father's tombstone. I hadn't made many visits to this site during the forty plus years since his passing. When I did visit, it was out of obligation. Over the years, I practiced keeping thoughts and feelings about my dad far from my mind. That morning, however, I felt compelled to make an appearance at the cemetery.

"Here we go, water for the flowers and a screwdriver to dig out the metal vase." My husband, Keith, had dropped me at the graveside, parked the car, and brought the necessary equipment to decorate the grave.

"What's wrong?" Keith asked when I made no acknowledgment of his return. "I thought you wanted to come here today."

"I thought I did too. But when I got here, all the old feelings of resentment and fear of this man that I barely knew came flooding back. Then some woman in a red dress declared him a hero," I snorted.

Keith went about adorning the grave with multicolored irises. I watched him in silence until he finished.

"Do you want to go now?" he asked.

"No, I want to just sit here for a few minutes."

It was a warm day with a slight breeze moving shadows of leaves from the massive tree that grew a few feet from my father's grave. I watched the lady in red walking among graves and placing flags. I thought about what she said, wondered why she spoke to me and how she knew anything about my father. I didn't even know very much about him.

"Maybe it was a mistake to come here, Keith. I didn't know much about this man other than he had a bad temper that erupted at the slightest provocation." I directed my remarks to my husband but kept my eyes on the grave.

"Maybe you just don't remember the good things about him. Maybe it's time you stopped hating your father and made peace with the past. What did she say?" Keith asked.

He nodded in the direction of the red-clad stranger.

"She said these men and women sacrificed their health, even mental health..." I trailed off and gasped.

"Where did your dad serve, Laura?"

I whispered the answer as I let out my breath. "Northern Africa. He was a munitions expert on the front lines. He always said his hearing wasn't right because of explosions and yells from his fellow soldiers that were injured or..." again words failed me.

"Keith, do you think my dad had PTSD and that was why he had such erratic and violent outbursts? I know he died from a service-connected disability in his fifties, after decades of suffering. But do you think what they once called 'shell shock' was the major factor in Papa's mental instability?"

"I don't know, Honey. I think it's very likely. What else do you remember about him, besides his temper? Papa, is that what you called him?" Keith asked. I nodded.

I sat for several minutes allowing the warm breeze and sunshine breaking through the tree's shelter to form a safe place for unpacking memories. I shook my head to clear decades of mental cobwebs laced with resentment.

"Well, he had a great sense of humor and quick wit. He loved music and Ed Sullivan. He fancied himself quite the dancer. He and my mother went dancing a lot at the old Elitch's Trocadero Ballroom. They won quite a few contests, you know, and..." I seemed to be having trouble completing sentences.

"Wait a minute, here. Do you think that my love for, and gifts in, dance are due, in part, to Papa? I always thought it was my Celtic roots on my mother's side." Now I was just talking to myself more than Keith as truths soaked in about this gift which my dad was partially responsible for handing to me.

Papa's words about dancing floated up and around me like a comforting blanket. I laughed when I remembered him saying, "You know on the dance floor, I can forget everything but the music and the movement. I feel free and freed."

How could I have missed and buried this offering which my father had passed along to me? My resentments kept me from this precious memory and putting more pieces into the puzzle that was defining my life as an artist. How could I have missed this?

For the next two hours, we sat under the big tree as shadows shifted on and around us while I told Keith about my dad. I alternated laughter with tears and silence until I realized why I felt compelled to visit his grave.

Keith was right. It was time to begin the healing and understand that my father was not an angry, brutal monster. He had something no one diagnosed in those days—one of the effects of war—Post Traumatic Stress Disorder. He had no way of understanding nor controlling it. As we strolled through my childhood there were as many, or more, good memories as bad. Those memories were buried under years of anger, resentment, lack of understanding and even unprocessed grief.

As evening approached, Keith reminded me we had a dinner commitment. I reluctantly agreed to leave, but not before cleaning off my father's headstone and rearranging the irises. I stood for a few minutes searching the massive cemetery for the lady in red. She appeared to have vanished.

"Keith, did I tell you Papa's favorite flower was the iris? He grew them you know," I said.

"No, I didn't know that, Laura." Keith took my hand, and with tenderness, guided me toward the car. I turned to look back at the grave of Albert Carvallo, Tech 5, U.S. Army WWII Veteran. I saw the silent, accompanying inscription that would not be seen by others, but never forgotten by Private Carvallo's daughter: "Father, dancer, and giver of freedom on many fronts."

Through tears of new-found understanding, I thanked Papa for the gift of freedom that cost him his sanity, his health, and ultimately his life. I told him that I am carrying on the tradition of dancing in and for release. For the first time, I saw my father as a true hero.

I have since cried many tears of loss and released my resentment toward my dad. I have processed where our country would be without the brave men and women in uniform who selflessly sacrifice to protect and defend our freedoms. And I have acknowledged that even from his grave that day, Papa gave me a new kind of freedom that is only found in the reconciliation of forgiveness, recognition, and gratitude.

There are still many things I don't, and probably will never, know about the man I called, "Papa." This I know for sure: future visits to the final resting place of my father will no longer be out of obligation.

Today's Prayer

Father, thank you for my earthly parents, the gifts they gave to me which, in my father's case, were many. Help me always dance with his love of dance and freedom in my feet and heart, out of honor to him and obedience to you.

Little Drummer Girl

Listening to the One who loves me

"Dance is absolutely not an appropriate art for worship. It is almost indecent to think about dancing in church. And on the altar? No, my dear, no."

Like so many others in church, I was seeking permission from the leaders to bring my gift from the Lord in prayer, praise, and worship. This strong rebuke left no room for discussion and no margin for doubt. My gift was not wanted nor recognized as a valid worship art.

I went home and prayed about my encounter and asked God to erase my dream of dancing with and for Him. After a few weeks, I submitted to the words of the church elders and accepted the fact that my art was not altar-worthy.

For months I tried to bury the dream of dancing with and for God's people. I even questioned Him about the reminders He sent in dreams and visions when I heard praise music and my favorite hymns. My mind always saw a dance. My feet refused to be still, and my heart flooded with praise in the movement.

Then one Christmas, I was listening to music on the radio, and I heard the song, "The Little Drummer Boy" (Lyrics by Katherine Kennicott Davis, 1941).

The song is about a child who felt his gift was not worthy of the new king. Still, he was encouraged to bring his gift to the cradle of the Baby Jesus and to give his very best.

I closed my eyes and listened to the story of the small, fictitious boy who brought his gift forward and offered what he had to our Lord. He played his best for Jesus, emphasizing his praise with every heartbeat, "Pa rum pum pum-pum" Oh how I identified with the little boy—shy, small, and convinced he had gift poverty. But God said, "Bring your gift child, bring your gift."

"I have no gift to bring
Pa rum pum pum-pum
That's fit to give our King
Pa rum pum pum-pum"

My hurting heart heard the words and understood that no matter what anyone said, God defines "worthy"; and all His gifts are worthy. I committed that day to always dance for an audience of One first. I surrendered my gift to Him knowing He approved it, and He would use what He gave me at His designated time. I just needed to keep dancing for and with Him. I agreed to obey His command despite directives from the powerful people within churches.

"I played my drum for Him
Pa rum pum pum-pum
I played my best for Him
Pa rum pum pum-pum
Rum pum pum-pum
Rum pum pum-pum
Then He smiled at me
Pa rum pum pum-pum
Me and my drum."

In the stillness, I knew the time would come for dance to be brought into worship. And it wasn't long before it was.

Since then, I've danced from California to Ottawa in praise to Jesus. I've been in big churches and small, retreats and workshops—as teacher and student. God has used this gift to bless, heal me and encourage others as each step brings glory to Him. He has asked one thing of me and that is to relinquish the approval of others in exchange for the opportunity to honor Him through obedience.

I never stop thanking Him for that moment when He used a secular tune to comfort and encourage me in His plans. There are few mornings, after awakening, when I don't walk into the presence of my favorite dance partner. He always takes me in His arms and we move together in prayer and praise as I hum, "Pa rum pum pum-pum."

Today's Prayer

Lord, thank you for gifts given to me and to everyone. Help me to always rest in your truths, even if the world says otherwise. To ignore your words in favor of seeking approval and accolades from humans is to practice disobedience.

I Am a Dancer

I am a dancer
What's that you say?
I'm too old, not thin
You can't see me that way?

Well, my daddy says
He made me to dance
I have never known Him
to anoint folks by chance

His call was in late life
when I heard Him say
"Twirl and spin love
as you praise and you pray"

So, no matter what
I obey His strong call
I know I can trust Him
to not let me fall

I am a dancer
What's that you say?
I don't have your permission
Well, hey, that's okay

To God I'm on pointe
and gold medals I've won
No matter who watches
My audience is of One

His plan is for joy
and He shares that with me
He asks me to share His
joy with others, you see

To disobey my father
I do not plan to do
He gave me this gift
to share with you too

I am a dancer
What's that you say?
Why yes, it is likely
*He sees **you** in that way*

So, grab my hands
let your heart be free
And you can say
you too are like me

We are dancers
What's that you say?
It's a delightful dessert
and a joy to obey

Move into His light
to twirl and spin
He's trying to show us
in Him we're all kin

Final Author Notes

When I graduated from high school in 1969, I had a dream of being the first in my family to complete a college education. There was one problem, I read at a fourth to sixth grade level. One might ask, and reasonably so, how I made it out of high school and into college. Let's just say there are distinct advantages to being raised in a family where one perfects skills needed to slip and trip, shuck and jive and basically get by, to survive and thrive. This is a story for another time.

Having received messages that I could not and would not ever read, I made the choice to own that as my reality for decades. Then I met the risen Christ who provided a mentor in the form of a woman named Dolores. She taught me that, with prayer, reliance, hard work, and perseverance, I could, and would, realize my dreams and much more. "Could and would," became the new reality I donned as a cloak of self-identification.

I do give God the credit for bringing this screaming and kicking little spiritual refugee (me) into the light of His promises. He used humans too. Due in large part to Dolores, (the subject of my first book *Dolores, Like the River*), a supportive, loving husband as well as my lifetime best friend, my sister Mary, I have been able to see those dreams, and more, come to fruition. Today I hold an MA in storytelling through creative movement and have published three books, including this one. It has been a blessing to be published by

Chicken Soup for the Soul and in a variety of other publications and to have earned multiple awards for my stories and my book *Jesus in Shorts.*

Storytelling is in my genes and inherited from a very imaginative, vivacious Celtic mother as well as a clever Sicilian father. I realized early on, however, that my gifts for storytelling, writing and dancing were not given for the purpose of allowing me an exaggerated image of self. God's intention in my gifting, as in the gifting of all His kids, is to encourage others on their journey to see that they too can and will see their dreams in real time.

For these gifts, I am eternally grateful. I offer praise and thanksgiving for the garnishments that make my days attractive and palatable, the surrender that makes me more teachable, the rich application of my life's lessons and the sweet desserts awarded from bending my will into obedience to His.

Life is a feast that He has created and is offering us. Come to His table and don't settle for less than all four rich courses.

About the Author

Laura Padgett is the daughter of a first-generation Sicilian-American father and a fourth generation Scottish-Irish mother. Her rich, diverse ethnic background affords her opportunity to explore many gifts given by her ancestors including storytelling, dancing, and cooking.

She holds an MA from Regis University in Storytelling Through Creative Movement which she received at age fifty-eight. Since graduating, she has authored two books, *Dolores, Like the River: The Life-Altering Influence of a Mentor* and *Jesus in Shorts: Twenty-five Short Stories of Life-Changing Jesus Moments.* She is a sought-after public speaker on why all stories matter, perils of perfectionism and an assortment of other subjects found on her website listed below.

At age forty, suffering from chronic fatigue syndrome, she took the advice of a doctor and started exercising. The form of exercise she chose was Irish Step Dancing. She put on her first pair of Irish dance shoes, began dancing, performing, competing and later teaching. She has never looked back. At age 74, she continues to teach both Irish and Praise Dance in her community.

When COVID shut down all opportunities to speak about writing, hold book signings, or teach dance, Laura called upon the wisdom of her father (a WWII veteran) who taught her, "When the going gets tough, the tough get creative." She turned to a trusted friend and asked him to teach her how to develop a podcast. On her 70th birthday, she launched a podcast called, "Livin' What You're Given." This is also the name shared by her monthly blog. In 2025, Laura chose to suspend the podcast to concentrate on dancing, teaching, speaking, and writing again. In the true spirit of staying curious at every age and stage, she began harp lessons in 2024.

Laura lives in the beautiful mountain valley town of Montrose, Colorado, with her husband Keith. She is a mother, stepmother, and grandmother. She enjoys dancing, writing, cooking, fine wine, playing her harp Bridget, hiking and just chilling in the world of nature and all arts.

If you enjoyed this book, please consider giving a review on Amazon or Goodreads to call attention to this body of work so that it may be of benefit to others. If you wish to read more stories on her blog, order books, view her speaking topics, or contact her, please visit her website at www.lauralpadgett.com. Special discounts are available on quantity purchases by book clubs, corporations, associations, and others.

Also from Laura Padgett

Dolores, Like the River

In a time when the world appears to worship all things youthful, sometimes aging is seen as synonymous with diminished value and purpose. Dolores was sixty-five years old, had raised two children, taught hundreds, and was enjoying peaceful retirement years, with her life's partner, in a sleepy mountain town in western Colorado. Then she met Laura, who was in her mid-twenties. God had a purpose for bringing these two women together. As you follow the narrative of their thirty-five-year relationship, it may change the way you see beauty and purpose in aging.

Available at amazon.com, westbowpress.com, barnesandnoble.com, and lauralpadgett.com.

ISBN: 9781490814384

Sample Chapter from
Dolores, Like the River

Chapter 1
On the Run

"Are you out of your mind?" Lana, one of my friends and coworkers, sat in disbelief. I had announced my intention to move from the sprawling metropolis of Denver. My plan was to relocate to Montrose, a small town in the middle of a valley and farmland on the western side of the Continental Divide in Colorado.

She fired question after question. "What can possibly interest you in some little mountain town? What life can that place offer someone in her twenties with a good job? How can it compare with living in a city with limitless artistic, educational, and cultural benefits?"

"Look, I have already explained this," I replied patiently. "I need to get away from here, and I need a change, period. I have a job waiting for me there."

Frankly, I was getting weary of well-meaning people demanding explanations from me. I was over twenty-five years old. I didn't owe anyone anything. I made it this far without anyone's help, and I was fully competent to continue with my life. The interference and unsolicited advice were becoming intolerable.

"How will you move? How will you take your stuff over there?" She wanted to know some of the details. I found that encouraging.

"Well, that's where I am hoping for some help from my friends," I admitted. I was grateful Lana was moving away from inquiring about my motives and my sanity. The new conversational direction gave me opportunity to ask for her assistance. I was counting on the fact that Lana rarely resisted opportunities to participate in novel exploits.

I lit a cigarette and continued unfolding my plans. "I'm selling some belongings. The place I'm renting is fully furnished. My old Chevy will carry some of my worldly goods. Since you have a large van, I am asking you to transport the other things I plan to keep. I'll pay for gas and food."

"Okay," she said, "but why Montrose? What is over there that interests you? Laura, I'm going to miss you. It does sound like a fun adventure, but are you sure? I mean you just started back to school and are dating a cool guy. What about all that?"

"I don't think that relationship is what I really want; and as I keep saying, I need to get away from here and away from my mother. I've put up with her last hurtful stunt. I don't care if she is a drunk. That is her choice, and drinking has always been more important to her than her family. I just need to find my own life without worrying about bailing her out of jail or plucking her off the streets. I'm tired of the vomit, the drunken friends, and the midnight calls to rescue her. I've seen all the dumps on Larimer Street that I care to in this lifetime, thank you." I stubbed out one cigarette and lit another.

After a few minutes of silence, I stopped trying to persuade her. "Look, if helping me is a problem for you, forget it. I'll get there with what I can carry in my car," I said. I tried to make my voice reflect the resolve in my heart and gut. No one was going to stop this move.

"All right, I'll help you. But you still haven't answered my question. How did you decide on Montrose?" she asked.

I told her I answered an advertisement in a trade magazine for employment. When I went to the job interview, the little town looked like a perfect place for what I hoped would be a new start. It was small, quaint, in the middle of beautiful country, and 250 miles from my current home and my mother. Lana shrugged and again assured me she would assist with my move.

I was relieved. Moving was one thing, but leaving all my worldly belongings behind was something altogether different. For a moment, as I talked this through with her, I felt sadness for leaving my life in Denver, especially because my two sisters lived there. I couldn't think about that now. I had to go. I had to.

On the Saturday of my departure, several people, including my sisters, were there to help with the final loading. No one seemed to share my enthusiasm for my newly chosen direction. I put their feelings and objections aside. I was leaving, period. They could come and visit any time they wanted, or not.

The trip from Denver to Montrose took about five hours. I drove a 1950 Chevy sedan I had won in a bet when the Pittsburgh Steelers beat the Dallas Cowboys in the 1976 Super Bowl. My jalopy was loaded with records, stuffed toys, clothes, a few plants, and several cartons of Marlboro cigarettes. The rest of my worldly goods preceded me out of town, in the van.

I was born and raised in Denver, but my family spent little to no time playing in the nearby mountains. My father had a heart condition that made it difficult to breathe in higher altitudes. Denver's elevation, at one mile above sea level, was about all he could take in the years before his death at age fifty-six. My mother usually complained of motion sickness and didn't like traveling on the winding roads over mountain passes. For me, the mountain scenery was no more recognizable than it would have been to a first-time Colorado visitor.

There were, however, some familiar spots along the journey out of town. A memory of one picnic near the small town of Bailey, off Highway 285, came to mind. I remembered Papa coming to get me out of a tree when I climbed too high and cried for rescue. He laughed and teased me but had no problem responding to the pleas of his middle child. There were times my dad could be very tender and gentle. But I was hard-pressed to find a lot of those warm, fuzzy memories.

I thought there were probably some good things about being in a family but, personally, I had developed a preference for flying solo. Refusing to be melancholy about leaving Denver behind, I focused on the September landscape.

In the fall, Colorado high country is fantastic. The aspen trees dance on the breeze as they shamelessly swirl their multicolored frocks. Little creeks appear from time to time along the winding roads and add voices to nature's concert, in support of the trees' choreography. Copious amounts of green, gold, and brown wild grasses rustle in response to grazing by small and large creatures.

We made our way over Kenosha Pass and descended onto a long stretch of road running through Park County. The area is called South Park. This piece of land, for the most part, is flat and supports ranches. A keen eye can pick up the graceful form of an antelope sharing feeding ground with cattle and sheep. Fields are populated with an array of fall wild flowers. All this open space rests in the shadows of the rugged Rocky Mountains. Towering, treeless peaks sport snow caps that serve as headgear year-round.

The beauty caused my breath to catch in my throat. The doubts that incessantly played as background music in my mind were momentarily silenced. Truly, this was a good decision. This was the right decision.

Lana and I stopped to stretch our legs about halfway through the park. "This is like a completely different world. This is where you are going to live, Laura. Maybe this isn't such a stupid idea after all. It's beautiful," she announced.

"Yeah, thanks. I know. But this isn't exactly my destination. That's over a pass or two yet," I informed her.

She didn't hear me. She was busy snapping pictures in every direction. I pulled out a cigarette, lit it, blew out the match, and put the spent fire implement in my jacket pocket. My father had always said that careless humans were usually responsible for forest and wild grass fires. On the rare occasions when I found myself out of doors, my father's words served to keep me in proper ecological posture.

A different world was right. I hadn't seen so much open land in a very long time. The smell of the fields and the sight of the looming mountains were calming balm over my hesitant heart that waxed and waned between righteous certainties of my new direction and viewing each passing mile in the light of loss. I missed my sisters already. I felt guilty about leaving my mother without telling her what was going on or even calling to say good-bye. I took a long drag on my cigarette.

"She is not my responsibility. She chose her life. Let her live it. I am going to live mine," I said out loud to the silent and seemingly understanding mountain range bordering the park.

After we made our way through South Park, we climbed, crossed, and descended Monarch Pass. The forested areas held my attention and provided return to the positive swing of the pendulum of uncertainty. There was cleanliness about these surroundings. The aged pine trees exuded a strength that testified to their resilience and determination in the face of the severe Colorado winters. I hoped this pristine yet rugged environment would wash away my past.

Arriving in Montrose evoked delightful mutterings from my traveling companion. "Wow, this place is gorgeous. Can you just imagine all the pictures you can take? And look, there's a restaurant and everything," Lana observed.

"Good," I snarled. "I need a beer. I hope this place isn't dry."

The five-hour drive from Denver to Montrose was accompanied only by soft drinks as liquid sustenance. Drinking and driving terrified me. The memories never seemed to fade of the accidents and DUIs my mother had racked up, not to mention expenses for bailing her out of jail. Then there were the court appearances. But that was all behind me now. She could bail herself out, appear before judges solo, and deal with her own accidents and the financial disasters resulting from her choices. I was free—free from her and free from my past. She couldn't hurt me now.

Lana and I ate, drank, and then found the little apartment I was renting. After unloading my car, we took off in the old Chevy to explore the town. To our delight, there were several bars and dancing establishments.

"This will do nicely," I said. "This will do nicely, indeed."

The next morning, Lana headed home, but not before I treated her to breakfast at one of the local greasy spoons. During breakfast, she said it seemed like I already knew my way around and was going to do just fine.

I let her leave without telling her that I, in fact, had been to Montrose while in high school for a sporting event. She didn't need to know that my parents were from Grand Junction, just an hour north, and that on trips to the Junction my family had driven through this little spot many times. It wasn't important to inform her that this was a frequent trip for my father and his three daughters when he needed to deposit us for a few weeks with family while he searched for our wayward mother. Although Montrose was to be my new home, returning to Grand Junction with its memories of fear and abandonment did not factor into my plans.

After breakfast, I watched my friend drive toward the highway leading back to Denver. I tried to silence the sad, little voice protesting that the last contact to my old life was heading back to the Mile High City without me. The seesaw of feelings, with positive affirmation on one side and guilt with trepidation on the other, was getting old. I swallowed hard and reminded myself I was finally free. That was the biggest positive imaginable in my book.

After waving to Lana's rear view mirror, I lit a cigarette, popped the top on a fresh beer, and walked into my new life.

www.ingramcontent.com/pod-product-compliance
Lightning Source LLC
LaVergne TN
LVHW051352080426
835509LV00020BB/3397